CHAPTER 1

How it started

How it all started

I t was early winter in 2015 and an old Army friend called Mick Ingham got in touch. He'd been following trips that I'd done for RMT Motorcycle Training to France and Portugal via Facebook, asked me to organise a trip for him and a club he was associated with called 'Castaways'. They were a bunch of misfits who'd broken away from another motorcycle club - probably been booted out!

They were all into riding their bikes, did their own thing, had no riding rules as a club, and usually got split up or lost every time they went out for a group ride. They wanted to go to Normandy in France 2016 to celebrate D Day and I was only too happy to help. I found out that the Chateau Le Mont Epinguet, near Cherbourg (a quaint and very old chateau that I had previously used on a number of occasions), was available for the dates they wanted to go.

Numbers confirmed, things booked, including the ferry, it was just a matter of time before we'd meet up in Portsmouth for the departure to Caen. Mick, who I hadn't seen since 1986 had also invited some old Army friends called Fletch and Ginge, whom I hadn't seen since around the same time. It was going to be our own little '13 Squadron, 8 Regiment, Royal Corps of Transport (RCT)' reunion.

Unfortunately, when we arrived at the ferry, we were informed that Mick, who'd instigated the tour wasn't able to make it as his wife had an eye problem and needed an operation. So Fletch turned up alone and as he didn't know anyone else in the Cast-aways felt a bit out on a limb, but was made to feel welcome by everyone and fitted in straight away.

As Ginge lived in Germany, he was going to ride down during the day to meet up with us in France the following morning, once the ferry arrived in Caen, as it was an evening ferry crossing.

True enough, Ginge was waiting as we disembarked. We'd had a few text exchanges to ensure he was in the right place to meet up and when we rode out of the port he was ready and waiting to join the group.

A quick "hello" and a with a fist shape we touched knuckles as a greeting. There was some shouting of "how you doing and great to see you" over the engine noise of the bikes and we were on our way without stopping. Pegasus Bridge was our first opportunity to talk to one another and have a proper catch up. It was funny when Fletch remembered Ginge as 'The nice Corporal'.

It wasn't long before we were back to our old banter with each other, as if all the years hadn't been between our last meeting and this one. We told each other of our military days and what had happened to us since being in civvy street.

Ginge was a self employed financial advisor with a very nice passive income, and Fletch was now a serving police officer on the bike unit in Essex. I'd left the Army in 1996 and started my own business running a motorcycle training school in Redditch, Worcestershire. I'd had an employment opportunity in Hull, where my girlfriend lived at the time and had enjoyed my early months of civilian life in Yorkshire, before the hard slog of setting up a new business from scratch.

It was great to catch up and we enjoyed each other's company for the remainder of the trip. It was apparent that Ginge was well into his riding and 'stumpy' was his latest BMW R1200GS. He'd toured a few times and he'd also ridden to Africa and had a great time. He spoke about his new and latest challenge and that was a trip to Istanbul or somewhere else but I couldn't recall where, as the wine had been flowing extremely well as we chatted.

It wasn't until a few days later over a beer, that Ginge asked me if I'd like to join the trip that he was going to plan. It would be some time the following year. I'm sure he'd waited a few days to see if I could ride and I reckon he was checking me out before offering the invitation. Of course I said yes I was interested, as trips like that, with decent guys don't come your way very often.

So, I had now registered my interest but I had lots to sort out if I went. I'd need a new bike, have to sort out work and have enough time off to be able to do the trip justice. I had said yes but didn't think anymore of it, and certainly at that time just thought Ginge was being polite by inviting me, as when he'd mentioned it I must have looked interested.

I was interested in doing a big motorcycle trip and something that not many people actually have the opportunity to do. I was proficient at riding abroad and had done regular trips to France, Spain and Portugal, but this was a whole new animal to me and the chance of a lifetime.

The 'phone call'

In late March 2017, I received a phone call out of the blue from Ginge. "Right all systems go, are you ready for the trip?"

Oh My God, it wasn't just a drunken invitation, he meant business! I went along with the phone call saying that I was interested but I really needed to get lots sorted out before I could commit properly. And besides I didn't have the right kind of bike to be joining the tour, as there was talk about off road sections in Albania and possibly other places too.

I had said yes of course, but not really been 100% committed because I wanted to do it but was not in a great position to be able to. I had a Kawasaki ZZR1400 motorcycle and not an adventure bike that would be needed for this journey. I had a business that was just about ready to launch (or so I thought) and a motorcycle training company that still needed some of my time, even though I had a manager manning the fort.

Our discussion was to sort out a prospective timeframe. I was doing a tour to Portugal mid to end of May with a group of people, so there was no way the trip to Asia could be before that as we were almost in April now. July and August would be far too hot for riding in Eastern Europe and would be extremely uncomfortable and Ginge couldn't do September as he had a wedding to attend.

I was informed that a guy called Mike Whitehouse would be going too. He was an old friend of Ginge's from 8 Regiment RCT in Münster Germany. Mike had been there from 1976 to 1981 and Ginge from 1980 to where his time overlapped with mine when I arrived in 1985. So Ginge was the common denominator here as he knew both of us, but at different times.

Mike hadn't ridden a bike for some years and had recently purchased one ready for the trip, he was busy getting some miles in, to get used to riding it. I didn't know Mike, but by the end of 3 weeks, we'd get to know each other pretty well and being ex squaddies at 8 Regiment RCT, had lots in common anyway.

8 Regiment RCT had been a very difficult unit to be in as a young and new soldier. A tough place and not for the faint hearted, demanding at times and extremely hard for even the toughest of young men. We'd work hard and play even harder whenever we got the chance.

Mike had to be back by early July so by the powers of elimination we concluded that June would be the best time to go. Early June it was going to be but it couldn't be until after 5th June, which was my wedding anniversary and being as I wasn't usually around for it, I'd said I would be for this one. So the date was set for the 6th or 7th June for Mike and I to leave the UK and meet up in Emsdetten, Germany with Ginge before the long journey southbound to Asia.

Right, now to start worrying about how I was going to get ready for such a huge trip in June, after a two week tour to Portugal in the last 2 weeks of May. There would only be a one week gap between arriving back from Portugal and departing for Istanbul. At the beginning of May I made the decision to go, and had just under three weeks before my departure to Portugal, things were going to be a little tight to say the least!

Meeting at Mikes House

Less than 2 weeks after the first phone call (mid April), we had our first meeting with all three of us together at Mike's house. Ginge had travelled over from Germany on his way to Bridlington (to visit family) and detoured slightly to give his presentation of the trip to date.

We arrived around 10:00 am for a cup of tea and a hearty breakfast and had a quick catch up on what we were all doing now. There was lots of reminiscing about old times and who we each knew or remembered from our army times, before getting on with the main agenda.

Ginge had a very well prepared presentation in true military style, I think he still prefers to be called Corporal Dooling to be honest! He gave a full overview and general outline of the tour (with pictures and humour) before breaking it down into the outward and inward prospective routes and distances.

The only objective for Ginge was to ride to Asia, take some happy snaps and get video footage before starting the route back. He advised that 'Top Gear Rules' would be applied to the trip, which meant that if you broke down you were on your own. This was fairly normal for this type of trip, although you wouldn't be left alone until you were sorted out or had help at hand.

During the outbound trip Mike and I were to head over to Emsdetten to meet up with Ginge, stay the night at his place and head south to Austria the following morning. This was going to be two big days riding, Ginge would lead the first and second days routes, as that would be heading south through Germany and he already knew the roads. Then we'd ride over the Gross-glockner Pass in Austria which he'd also ridden before.

Then on a rotational basis we'd do a route each per day after that, so that we'd have a day leading and two days off. That way we could choose our own routes and things to do, in each of the countries we were travelling through.

It was at this stage that I said I was only 90% sure I would be going ahead with the trip. I didn't have time to do any routes or preparation, as I was extremely busy at work at this precise moment in time. Because of this I said don't rule me in properly but don't rule me out either, if I'm in I'll tag on and if I'm out then you won't be left in the lurch with unplanned routes.

The route would be through Slovenia, Croatia, Bosnia, Albania into Greece and then finally Istanbul in Turkey. Once in Turkey we'd go across the Bosphorus River and into Asia. Then we'd turn around and ride back via Bulgaria, Romania, Hungary, Pol-and and then back into Berlin in Germany to finish the tour, and back at Ginge's for a late afternoon cup of tea!

Both Ginge and Mike said they'd take the responsibility to or-ganise the routes each day, as they both had lots more time on their hands than I did. I said I'd be happy leading a few routes if they gave me the sat nav gpx file prior to leading a particu-lar day, I was more than happy to help out with navigation and leading, to give the others a break. But I didn't want to say I could do the route planning if I didn't have time, or worse still not be able to go at all.

We ended the meeting with a good brief and continued to dis-cuss the finer points on our recently opened WhatsApp Group. This was to become the main source of communication for the tour.

As I hadn't met Mike before this meeting, I said I'd pop over to spend an hour or two with him so that we could get acquainted and not be complete strangers before embarking on a tough journey. He only lived an hour or so away from me, so it was a good reason to try out my new bike that I'd have to purchase for the trip.

How we all knew each other

Mike is about 10 years older than me, around 60 years of age and Ginge is halfway between us both. He was posted to 8 Regiment in the late 70's to early 80's. Being in a Corps in the Army meant that you didn't move from place to place as a unit like Infantry Battalions did, instead the unit stayed where it was and the soldiers got posted in and out every 3-4 years.

Ginge arrived at 8 Regiment in the early 80's as a new recruit. Mike had already done his time there and was an old sweat (which meant that he was well established), was well known and had a certain amount of respect for the time he'd already done. These guys tended to guide the younger, more inexperienced soldiers and it was how the knowledge was passed down, with their education and the odd slap to keep newer, younger soldiers in check.

It was a very tough unit to be in as a young man on his own in a new environment. 8 Regiment RCT had a very close working relationship with the local American Army, our role was to support them and carry their nuclear warheads around Germany during the Cold War. We worked hard and played even harder in those days, young men without any real responsibilities and pretty free spirits really.

By the time I arrived in 1985 Mike was long gone and Ginge was now one of the old sweats and I was one of the 'NIG's' who had just been posted in. Being 'New In Germany' gave you the nickname NIG, until a new lot of young unsuspecting and naive guys were posted in. So the common denominator of the trip was Ginge, he had known Mike from the early 80's and then knew me from the mid 80's. Our (Mike and I) paths had never crossed as he'd been and gone many years before my time. In fact I was still at first school when Mike was posted to Münster in Germany where 8 Regiment RCT was based.

Both Mike and Ginge had worked hard since leaving the Army, they had both been in the financial advice business and had been very successful in their civilian careers. I felt like the poor relation when they talked about their salaries and what kind of money was involved in the passive incomes that they both enjoyed.

Perhaps I went into the wrong game when I left the Army! I am not saying they'd had easy lives, things just looked pretty good for them right now.

CHAPTER 2

Getting ready for the off

Getting ready for the adventure

I left the meeting with a lot of excitement but also trepidation and a lot of anxiety. I didn't have a bike, I didn't have any kit, I wasn't prepared in any way, shape or form to embark on such a trip. It was going to be hard graft, getting ready for 2 tours within a month, sorting out any business issues and having the time to get away.

The training business was in good hands, there was a manager and some good trainers in the company. It was well established and just needed to tick over really. There weren't many problems that could arise that hadn't happened before, so I took the opinion that it was in safe hands with the office staff being brilliant at what they did.

The new business venture that I was working on was Video-Biker, it was still in its pre-launch stage. I'd done pretty much everything I could do on my part and at that precise moment in time was just waiting for my partner to get the website launched, so that we had a working business. Because the timeframe wasn't imminent I made the decision that I could take the time out without causing too much stress and with this trip being a chance in a lifetime, my mind was made up (nearly).

The problem now was finding a decent enough bike that would do the journey and get me there and back. My budget wasn't huge as I'd be dipping into savings to embark on the trip. I needed a bike first, so without wasting any time or money on other stuff I needed to purchase the bike. I would use my Kawasaki ZZR 1400 for the Portugal trip and this would give me some room for movement to find a bike in the week between Portugal and Asia. This decision was far from ideal but if needs must, I was looking to get a bike at around the £5000 mark (which was my budget), but I'd have to do a bit of searching.

I called a few dealers that I knew and there were loads of these bikes for sale, lots were quite expensive as they were only a few years old. They were big money which I wasn't prepared to spend for just one trip. I'm not an adventure bike rider and never have been. I like to try a bike properly before deciding on such a big expense. I needed to decide which bike I wanted, the GSA or the GS, and I didn't know if the guys I was going away with had the big or smaller tank.

A few messages later I found out it was one of each, that settled it for me. Ginge would be filling up every 150-200 miles so I'd opt for the smaller tank too. The bikes were also much cheaper by going for this option. Then I had to make a decision on luggage, what I really needed and what could I get away with. Many bikes came without luggage and a few had the lot, up to £1000 difference because of luggage on the R1200GS. This was not going to be an easy choice, I'd have to research, find one and go for it as it seemed everyone had the same idea.

I wondered why there were so many for sale, was it because they were too big as a normal bike? Do people like the idea of doing an adventure but never really do one? Is the bike considered as a toy, just to say you've got one or are they that big people are frightened of them and find them difficult to ride and manoeuvre? Lots of unanswered questions, but all I kept hearing was that they were brilliant bikes!

I popped into Arden Motorcycles in Alcester as I usually did for the training business, either to pick stuff up that had been ordered or take a bike in for repair. I stood at the counter and asked Simon if he knew of or had heard of a BMW R1200GS for sale. He looked at me a bit oddly and said, "What, like the one behind you!" I turned around and saw the bike, a blue/grey 1200GS with the luggage, on an 05 plate with a good service history and clean for its age. Arden had looked after the bike for the previous owner and it hadn't been ridden since he bought it and it had just had a full service.

The only thing I needed to do now was sort out the cost and the payment and whether the owner was going to sell it, as I was told that he wasn't really that bothered about selling it. I put in my offer, very close to the asking price because it was so tidy and had everything I needed for my trip. The offer was accepted, so I made a bank transfer immediately to secure the purchase and started thinking about getting the bike and the rest of my gear ready for the trip.

I decided to have the rear final drive bearing replaced as I'd heard they can give problems around 45,000-50,000 (ish) miles. I didn't fancy getting down to the bottom of Eastern Europe and needing the final drive bearing replacing. It could take a while to sort out and then there would be the added cost, because I'm a tourist who needs it repairing to get back home.

The bike had a full service a year earlier, it hadn't done any mileage since and had now got a full MOT. I decided to use the bike to go on the Portugal Tour to test it out and make sure it would do the job on the second journey forecast for Asia. I would rather break down in Spain or Portugal than Hungary, Romania or Albania!

Testing the bike out

The decision to go to Portugal on the bike wasn't an easy one, I was happy on the Kawasaki ZZR 1400 and it was a much quicker bike. Sometimes a bit of extra speed or acceleration is needed to get back in touch with the group if you've dropped off slightly or if you need to get back to the front for whatever reason. Another instructor would ride the Kawasaki and I would put the BMW through its paces to ensure it was up to the job for Asia.

The BMW didn't need anything doing to it for the first trip but I'd booked it in for a full service, tyre change and check over as soon as I returned. But on checking over the bike before the Portugal trip, it was found that the rear top box rail was sheared at the base of the lug that attaches to the rear frame. This ended up being a mammoth task and needed drilling and tapping. The tap sheared too which caused even more aggravation, the chisel also broke which meant a new part had to be machined on the lathe.

The mechanic Neil Bolton from NB Services was an absolute star and repaired the bike at extremely short notice. He also gave it a thorough going over and booked the bike in on the bank holiday Monday, for a full service and tyre change which was only a week before my departure for Asia.

During the Portugal trip, the bulb light kept going on and off and the brake failure light came on a few times, which meant the brake servo stopped working and the brakes became difficult to operate. It would sort itself out if I stopped, turned the engine off and reset the system but this was not an ideal scenario that I would accept on a 5000+ mile journey to Istanbul and back.

A guy I know who has ridden a R1200GS for years, did some research through a forum he was part of. He said he'd read that the brake servo and braking system should be bled to eliminate the problem of brake failure, the servo also continued to work after the front brake was released. The fault here was a corroded connection at the brake light switch, my guess was the bike had been stood for too long, it needed a good ride and the faults sorting out by a qualified mechanic.

It didn't cause any issues on the trip to Portugal, it was just annoying that these fault codes were occurring and I was hopefully heading to Asia on the bike in a few weeks time. I logged all the faults and reported them back to Neil when I arrived home. He was ready and waiting with all the stuff that had been ordered, collected and dropped off with him by one of my training instructors.

I arrived home from Portugal at almost midnight and was due

to be with Neil at 07:00 am the following morning. First I had to go to the office to collect a couple of things, so it was an early start. I arrived at Neil's and he was ready to get going straight away, he asked what faults I'd come across and got stuck in immediately.

The brake system needed bleeding from the servo as well as from the caliper, meaning it had new fluid in the whole system, both front and rear, the clutch fluid was also changed. The tyres were changed, although there was still plenty of life in them, I wanted new rubber and the bike had a full engine service ready for the big trip. The engine oil was still clean from previously but I wanted it and the oil filter changing all the same.

The bike was now ready to go to Istanbul but during that week whilst riding it, a fault code kept showing on the dash. It was the rear tail light bulb on the display, Neil wasn't available so I took it to Arden. Nick plugged it in on the diagnostic machine and investigated the rear light cluster, he must have moved something as the fault code disappeared. I was informed by many people, including mechanics, that this particular model had faults with the canbus system and nearly always showed a fault code. If you can't see anything wrong, just ignore it and carry on was the advice! I wasn't too happy about that but when a mechanic suggested covering up the warning code with some tape, I realised this was extremely common.

The bike was now ready for the trip, just a few bits to purchase for camping and for the possibility of any breakdowns or punctures and I'd be ready to go.

Loading the bike

What do I take? This is always a hard question, especially for new travellers as they always take too much stuff with them. They take everything they can possibly fit on the bike and fall just short of taking the kitchen sink.

Unless you dump stuff during the journey, you will never be able to load your bike the same as just before you leave. The reason is, that in the comfort of your own home, you can tightly pack everything and fit more than you need into panniers. Taking a female pillion is far more demanding, especially for their changes of clothing and matching accessories that need to be different every evening (tongue in cheek of course - lol). So it was a good job I didn't have a pillion passenger, the fact was, I wasn't taking a passenger anyway!

The way I pack for a big journey is as follows:-

Tank bag

I put valuables in my tank bag, along with things I'm going to need that day and some electric items too. I have my passport, driving licence and vehicle documents to hand for going through passport control if travelling through borders.

My waterproofs are close to hand (2 piece gore-tex walking gear that are more expensive in comparison to biking stuff but I find much better) with possibly a spare pair of gloves in case it rains. A few tools, like a screwdriver and pliers lurk at the bottom of the bag with a roll of electrical tape.

In their own little bag are electrical charging leads and adaptors for Europe. I carry a 2 meter phone charger cable which I use on the bike, a smaller one for when I arrive at my destination and a mini USB lead to charge other electrical devices. I even carry a portable battery pack in case I need an emergency charge. All of these items can be plugged straight into the bike's USB charger.

A bottle of water, ear plugs, spare ear plugs, visor cleaning kit with an E-cloth, 2 meter wire rope to secure helmet and clothing to the bike and a side stand puck. The plastic rain cover also lives in its own compartment along with waterproof outer mittens for extreme weather and cold. Finally I carry a packet of painkillers, sun cream if it's hot, lip balm along with anything else I might need, which could be a silk top just in case it gets cold during the ride.

On top of the tank bag I carry a map of the area I'm riding at the time, along with a notebook and a couple of pens. The sat nav, if I use one, would be on display, with a handwritten simple route card for the day. The sat nav case would also be close to hand as it doesn't stay on the bike when left unattended. The tank bag also has a combination lock. It isn't brilliantly secure but it stops unwanted people from unzipping it quickly.

Clothing

If I'm catching a ferry or know I'm only doing a flying visit, like arriving late in the evening and leaving first thing, I'd have some sort of overnight kit. It would either be in the tank bag or its own small overnight bag, that way I would not be carting all my belongings off the bike. They would stay on the bike securely, either in a locked top box or panniers.

I would also carry 5 to 6 pairs of underwear, along with the same amount of t-shirts, a couple of long sleeve tops, a short sleeve shirt or two and a hoodie or warmer top just in case it was cold.

I would usually wear a clean t-shirt in the evening after a shower and use it the following day along with the same underwear. I'd be banking on stopping in a hotel that will turn laundry around overnight to refresh my clothing. Or if stopping in one location, say an apartment, I'd wash my own stuff for the return journey or for the next phase of the tour.

Breakdown equipment

From previous motorcycle tours and knowing the kind of things that can go wrong, I carry a fairly comprehensive toolkit. Also part of the armoury is several ways of sorting out a puncture, rubber plugs along with the tools, green slime that blocks holes and as a final result a small can of tyre weld. I always carry radweld because I've seen two radiators leak whilst touring abroad.

The tools consist of various sized spanners, ratchet with sockets, assorted screwdrivers and pliers, a small hacksaw with cable ties, electrical and duct tape. Spare bulbs and rubber gloves with a small tube of hand cleaner. There are other useful bits and bobs in the tool kit but these items are down to preference and space. An air compressor is strongly advised between the group.

Camping gear

Camping isn't something I usually do on a trip but if you want a decent night's sleep, you will need to think about how much space you have and how much you are willing to carry.

A tent is a big consideration, it needs to be big enough for you and your valuables, tank bag, clothing, helmet and anything else you want to put in the tent overnight. The rest of your stuff left outside of the tent needs to be secure, there is nothing worse than having something stolen whilst you are sleeping!

A good sleeping bag that will keep you warm on a chilly night, a good air mattress for comfort and some kind of pillow if you are used to having one. I've never carried cooking equipment with me because it means cleaning and messing around when you could be up and off to a local place for coffee and a bite to eat. If you are on a camp site, they usually cater for the basics anyway.

A camping holiday is certainly different to touring big miles, I would have a plate and a knife and fork though, just in case I wild camped and had purchased some food from a local supermarket before stopping at the end of the day.

All of my camping equipment fits in its own bag which means it stays together and gets strapped to the back of the bike. The bag will fit into the pannier or top-box when stopping at a hotel for security.

What to wear and carry

Depending on the location of the trip and the weather conditions that are forecast, I prefer to wear two-piece leathers that zip together but if I'm travelling to hotter places, I'd opt for textile trousers and jacket, preferably that zip together too. The textiles will be vented with perforations to allow air to pass through to keep the body cool if its hot. But if it's cold, I'd bulk up on thin layers and wear my two piece waterproofs to keep my body warm, for comfort and concentration.

On my person I would usually carry my mobile phone but if it's being charged it would be powered up while it's in the tank bag. My wallet is always on me with my money and credit cards, it lives in a plastic bag most of the time. I may have some spare change lurking in one of my pockets along with the keys for the bike when I'm not riding.

Extras

Whatever your journey or tour, you will no doubt have something in mind that you personally want to do or achieve. I will always take a camera with me, it will either be the phone or a bigger camera for stills.

A video camera is also a must, my phone does pretty good off-the-cuff filming and so does the DSLR that I'd take if I have space. But I'd also take an action camera to capture on board footage.

Personally I prefer to use maps, they give a better representation of where you are, where you want to go and how you are going to get there. Most mobile devices do have decent maps now and at times I rely on a combination of sat nav, GPS location and a map on the phone or the good old fashioned paper map. The maps I carry are of the whole journey, the trip to Asia cost over £80 to purchase a map of each country we rode through.

There may be specific things that you personally need, for comfort or other reasons. So make sure they are essential and will be used, it's amazing how little you really need as most people don't use half of what they take with them anyway.

The final preparations

In the week between arriving back from the Portugal Tour and leaving for Turkey, it was just a matter of the final preparations to be ready for departure day.

I'd been over to spend an afternoon with Mike to have a catch up, as we'd not met since the briefing day. He was an old sweat and had left 8 Regiment before I arrived but he did know a chap named Tosh Ferrie and a few other people who I knew from AF-CENT in Holland. It's a very small world when you start talking to people about where they've been and who they know, peoples paths cross in mysterious ways.

I'd gone over my kit list a number of times and was busy laying it all out ready to pack. I use a kit list and place everything out on the floor or a spare bed and tick it all off. And then as I pack it, I ensure it's crossed off the list. The reason for this is if you get a bit blasé about packing what you normally take, you always forget something.

I know a chap who always goes through the same routine getting ready for a short flight back to the UK from Europe. He checks his house key, wallet, credit card and passport every time just before he leaves home. Only one time he knew his passport was there, as it always was but when he arrived at the airport after a train journey to get there, he couldn't fly because he didn't have his passport! It doesn't hurt to double check to make sure you have the important things with you, if you've got a passport you can travel and if you have a credit card you can purchase anything you've forgotten.

I usually lay the clothes out and wonder how I'm going to

live for so many days with so little stuff. But because you live in motorcycling clothes all day, you don't need much and it's going to be hot in south eastern Europe so shorts will do. Usually the clothes are worn for an evening meal and then taken off after a couple of hours, so they don't really get too grubby or dirty anyway.

The clothes are usually the first thing to get ready, I then go through my tank bag stuff to ensure all valuables are sorted out. This includes vehicle documents, insurance, breakdown cover, medical insurance and any phone numbers that might be needed. This time, without our partners knowing we added 2 contact details, one was our partners and the other was someone we knew just in case one of us was killed while away. We decided it would be better coming from someone who knew our partner, who would go round and tell them personally, rather than by a total stranger over the phone. Our partners knew the names of the people we were going away with but didn't know them personally and none had ever met.

Next was the bike repair kit and tools. Because I travel fairly often I have a container full of kit that I take with me, along with other useful items. It was just a case of a quick look over this stuff to make sure it was all there and re-acquaint myself with what I had. I didn't need to add anything to it except a new can of tyre weld as that had been used on a previous tour and I hadn't replaced it since.

Then the camping gear was next, I had to go and purchase a few items for the trip. So a couple of hundred pounds was spent getting ready for the odd night camping, of course you have to put the tent up in the garden just to check it's all there before your departure. There's no point getting there and finding stuff missing as it's too late then and you don't want to look stupid not knowing how to put it up either. Luckily everything was there and it was time to pack it up in the bag that would fit on the passenger's seat. Everything else was pretty simple really, after spending 13 years or so in the Army, a couple of overnight sleep outs in a tent could not be too difficult, or could it?

Then the DSLR camera, along with the 4k drift camera was going to be sorted out and the settings were changed so that video producer Calum Barre could edit the film when we got back. I took a day off to pop up to Shrewsbury to see him, he had a look at the cameras and adjusted the settings to idiot mode and I was under clear instructions not to change them. Then I just had to get as many micro SD cards together as I could, so that it would be easier to keep track of, produce and edit when I returned.

The bike was the final thing to get ready, it had been to the mechanic for a full service and one last look over, a few rides out on it was enough to give me the green light of satisfaction. I only needed my Euros now and I was ready for departure, the money is separated and put in different locations on the bike and around my body, so if I get robbed or the bike gets stolen I don't lose everything.

Always remember to have a second set of documents photocopied in case one set gets stolen and as a total backup on a web based email account that you can access from anywhere in the world. I have all my documents scanned and saved in a folder just in case I need to access them in an emergency.

And finally me, make sure I am well rested, feel ready to go and have any medication with me that I may need in case I'm in the middle of nowhere and need some tablets for something. Paracetamol, Anadin, Ibuprofen, Germolene, TCP and antibiotics all have a place in your first aid kit, if you usually need it, make sure you take it. Right, now I'm ready...

CHAPTER 3

England to Germany

Route planning

G oing touring means you're going to have to learn how to navigate, get to your destination and make your way home again. If you have never learned how to map read before, now is a good time to start to develop that all important skill of knowing where you are, where you are going and how you are going to get there.

First of all you have to decide on what kind of trip you are going to do. Is it a sightseeing trip? Do you want to have days off? Is it going to be big mileage each day? How many miles are you used to riding? Will you be using small side roads or main arterial routes? All these questions need to be answered at the planning stage before embarking on the journey.

Then you'll need to decide on a realistic destination, one that you can easily achieve and work out how many days you need to complete the trip. It is usual to encounter issues along the way, so always factor in some problems and delays. Don't set un-achievable targets for yourself or others.

There is no point trying to do 6-700 miles a day if you have never done this type of riding before. If you work on an assumption that you will only be covering around 50 miles in the hour for your days riding then you won't be far wrong. A full days riding around 7 hours will realistically achieve 350 miles on good roads.

Sat Nav

Too many people rely solely on one mode of navigation. Don't just simply follow the directions of a sat nav, learn how to use it, read the instructions and do some study or homework on what it can do. Practice using it, look at the menus and navigation conditions you can programme in. When you are on the move, you may need to change settings, it's a good idea to know what settings to use and how to change them quickly if you need to.

Most modern vehicles have built-in satellite navigation systems, they are widely used as a daily commodity even on short journeys, even though the driver knows the route. The use of them has become a way of life and 'by and large' are used as a comfort blanket, the only problem is, they are also heavily relied upon.

Does the sat nav know if it's been raining or there is a flood where normally a shallow ford is? Trucks and buses have been known to get stuck down narrow country lanes because the ignorant driver has gone where they are told to go and not used their brain.

Using a Garmin, TomTom or an alternative means of navigation on the bike is completely different. You are detached from the sat nav and don't necessarily have the voice to aid your navigation, unless it is Bluetooth and has been paired before departure.

Google Maps

Google Maps is a great way of planning and plotting routes, you can take your time and be in the comfort of your own home on the laptop or pc. Don't rush the planning stage, think about where you want to go and do some research to see if there is anything you should try to see in certain countries. Like a mountain pass that we were advised to do in Bulgaria on our return leg from Asia, by a young lady we met in Greece. Her named is Elena Graikou and she kindly gave her permission for me to use her picture on the rear cover of this book.

Because of the 'street view' it allows you to get right down to road level, look at critical points enroute and get a feel and mental image of certain places and junctions. It's a great heads up when you are looking for certain areas as you have a visual idea prior to arriving, it's almost as if you've been there before.

Maps

Old fashioned paper maps still have a major role to play when navigating new routes. They allow you to see the bigger picture, have detail on them without zooming in and at the planning stage you get a good overall visual feel of an intended area. Map reading can be a headache as not everyone is comfortable using a map, every rider should try to learn how to use one before going on their trip.

Route plans

Route plans are a good way of highlighting key towns to aim for, direction of travel and road names or numbers to look out for enroute. In conjunction with a map this can give you directions at a quick glance, you can also put a rough distance to each turn, so that you know it is getting closer and you can look out for the new road. You can come up with your own system or copy an existing method of route guidance.

Online or computer aids

There are some online navigation aids such as MotoGoLoco or Basecamp. These can take a bit of time to get used to using them but will give you good experience at plotting your own route. You will also be able to save routes as GPX files that the sat nav will be able to read.

In summary, whilst riding, I use a combination of a sat nav and other navigational aids and don't rely solely on one to get from A to B. There has been some real horror stories about sat nav routes that have been blindly followed. Using a combination of tools at your disposal is best, have a map in your tank bag that is visible on the road you are riding, with a simple route plan written down, and the sat nav as a guide or back up.

If in doubt stop and consult your map properly, and mobile phones are great at giving your exact position and location of the nearest roads or landmarks. It's also more interesting knowing where you are and where you are going, as getting lost or going in the wrong direction for miles adds hours to the days ride, reduces concentration levels and adds greater risk as fatigue sets in.

The Journey begins.

Day 1 - Redditch to Emsdetten (England to Germany)

Date: Tuesday 06 June 2017
Depart time: 06:40   **Arrive time:** 21:15

Start mileage on the motorbike 37,498 miles

Days Mileage: 510 miles
Fuel cost: £58.92 approximately and started with a full tank

Route:
Redditch (England) - Warwick service (meet up with Mike) - London - Folkestone - Eurotunnel - Calais (France) - Bruges - Ghent (Belgium) - Antwerp - St Nicholas - Venlo (Holland) - Duisburg (Germany) - Dortmund - Münster - Emsdetten

Roads:
Motorway all the way.

Border crossing:
Leaving England to enter into France passports were required and checked by Customs, bike documents were not checked. Leaving France, we were not checked again and all other borders were open and unmanned.

Weather:
Heavy rain in England, miserable and cold. Got extremely wet on the way to the EuroTunnel, arrived in France and it had dried up, very windy with very strong side winds. Continued through Belgium where it started to brighten up but was still cool, riding through Holland was the same and it started to warm up in Germany to a more pleasant temperature.

Countries travelled & Currency:

     England   Pound   £

	France	Euro	€
	Belgium	Euro	€
	Holland	Euro	€
	Germany	Euro	€

The Days Events - Time to go

Today's the day! I'd set the alarm clock for 05:30 am but there really was no need. I was awake on and off all night with anticipation and excitement. I was up at 05:15 am, well before the alarm had time to go off. The first thing I did was look out of the window to see a wet and windy start to the day and the rain was still falling pretty hard. I thought to myself, it's going to be waterproofs for the ride down to the Eurotunnel at least, but secretly I was hoping it would be brighter when we arrived in Europe.

After a shower I got ready and dug out the waterproof socks that I'd prepared the night before, just in case. I needed to wear waterproof socks because the boots I'd bought were perforated desert boots that were for the hot climates of arid Greece and beyond and not for the wetness of England. I suppose England is very green for a reason and that does not entail lots of hot sunshine and drought filled summers!

After a bite to eat I was ready, the bike just needed to be pushed out of the garage into the rain, a final check of passport, wallet, credit card and docs and I was ready to go. The passport was to make sure I could go abroad, the wallet because cash comes in handy, the credit card to purchase anything I'd forgotten to take and the documents so that I could pass through borders on the bike.

Riding in England

I was waved off at the front door at about 06:40 am and not before too long was on the M42 heading towards the M40 and

Warwick services, where I was meeting Mike at 07:00 am (ish). I thought this was a little bit too early to meet up but went along with it at the start of the tour, it wouldn't have been good to miss the first transport (train) that we'd booked at the very first hurdle. Besides, I couldn't have handled the piss taking from Ginge for the rest of the trip and I didn't really know how Mike rode either but would soon find out.

I arrived just after 07:00 am to find Mike at the services, he'd been there half an hour or so already. I thought he was either really keen or not too happy in the rain and as I greeted him I realised which one it was. He was going to despise the journey down past London in the rain and to the Eurotunnel. It wasn't long before we were on our way and I soon got the message that he wasn't happy riding in the rain at 60 mph, this was going to be a long ride. He had a dark visor on and a peak which blocked out too much light, he really lacked this kind of riding experience and these conditions were just added issues for Mike to deal with as we plodded south.

I soon got in front to lead the way and set the pace. We were travelling quite slowly and were being hit by all the spray in the middle lane, so I decided to ride at the same speed as the vehicles in lane 3 where possible, to minimise spray and keep up with traffic flow. We arrived at the M25 as the traffic started to get heavy and headed southbound towards Gatwick. The weather hadn't really improved at all, in fact it had gotten worse in places and now it was getting cold too. We arrived at a service station near Gatwick for a quick warm up and to fill up before the final 50 miles left to the channel tunnel exit on the M20.

The EuroTunnel

This was the first big mistake. We were both wet but Mike wasn't used to this type of riding. In fact he wasn't used to riding at all. It was a slow start in the rain and time seemed to be dragging on and on at 50-60 mph on the motorway. Granted it was raining pretty heavily but the speed was pitifully slow and we had been in the spray of the trucks for quite some time before the pace picked up. I really didn't want to push it too much at this early stage because I wasn't sure just how uncomfortable Mike was but it was going to be a long tour if this speed was going to be the norm!

The long break we took was really to get Mike comfortable and warm, but it really dragged on far too long and we needed to get on our way. We still had 400 miles to ride in total and needed to be at the terminal half an hour earlier than the 12:20 pm departure time for the train. It had taken almost 2 hours to get to the services and the 1.5 hour break we'd had might have been our biggest downfall and reason we could miss the train! Mike disappeared for at least 30 minutes, when he returned he told me he'd been drying his gloves in the toilets on the air blower. Oh dear, this really was going to be a long trip, I thought!

As we set off the weather improved slightly but we had to get a wriggle on to make the allocated time. I lead the way and made pretty good progress to get to the Eurotunnel on time. We arrived at the M20 and were soon up to speed and heading for junction 11a, still a bit wet and windy but as it had cleared slightly we were able to get a move on.

Upon arrival we went straight through passport control and ticket checks. A brilliant system really as you've already prebooked and checked-in, you are given a reference number and that's all you have to give to the person at the booth. We headed straight towards the waiting lines of vehicles and we were told that the train was a little bit delayed, which was a good job really as we were slightly late. We sat in line for no more than 10 minutes and were soon loaded onto the train.

We were guided towards the platform and shown the way onto the train from a side entrance. Once through the side door we rode up the train following the vehicles in front until they stopped. We parked our bikes at an angle and switched off, and that was us for the duration of the train journey. Almost as soon as we were on, we got our wet gear off and in no time at all the train pulled away from the platform and we were on our way for the 30-35 minute ride.

Riding in France

The time went really quickly and before we knew it it was light outside and we needed to get our skates on to be ready to disembark. As soon as I was fully dressed the train stopped, the doors opened and we were off. Straight out of the arrival area in Calais and straight onto the motorway. We were in France and heading north east straight towards Dunkirk along the coast road. The weather was much better, it had started to dry up but it was now 14:00 pm because of adding the hour's time difference. It was a bit chilly, damp roads in places and very, very windy.

Riding in Belgium

France was easy to navigate, continuing to follow the coast road up towards Bruges and turn right towards Ghent and into Belgium. Mike indicated to pull in after about 75 miles, I wondered what could be wrong but when we slowed down into the services he said it's time for a coffee. I told him he must be joking as we still had over 300 miles to go and that time was not on our side, I said we'd fill up and eat after another 100 miles and then get on with it or we'd never get there today! This was going to be one long adventure...

Because of the time it was fairly heavy traffic but still moving well, as motorways abroad tend to do because the driving discipline is much better and they move over after they have made an overtake. It was going too well and as we approached Antwerp it became congested and very quickly we found ourselves almost at a stand still with the rest of the traffic.

We filtered for about 20 miles. It was now hot and difficult riding as impatient car drivers were all over the place trying to see further ahead, not knowing what carnage was there. As we got to the front it was apparent why it was so bad. It was sheer carnage. There was an overturned truck with very little cab remaining and various other vehicles in different mangled states. We realised there had been a massive fatal accident. It's never good to encounter this kind of road traffic incident and even worse when you are so close that you can see it.

Riding in Holland and Germany

Once clear of the accident we were back to full speed and crossing the Dutch border in no time at all. It only took just over half an hour to reach the German border and I soon started seeing familiar road signs from 25 years previous when I was stationed in Germany, as a member of Her Majesty's Armed Forces serving in the Royal Corps of Transport (RCT).

Signs such as Venlo and Wankum on the German/Dutch border, then Duisburg, Düsseldorf and Dortmund. It wasn't long before we were heading north towards Münster on the Route 1 and then the Route 43. As we got closer, seeing the 'Münster Nord Ausfahrt' turning felt like returning home after many years of being away. This was the exit I used to take when going back to camp but today this wasn't our turning, we still had to go further north to Emsdetten.

The days destination

As we got closer, we used the sat nav to navigate to the petrol station where we'd been told we could fill up to ensure we had a full tank of fuel ready for an early morning start before finding our way to Ginge's house. We arrived late and behind schedule due to a number of issues. It had been a long day and one that we really didn't want to repeat during the next phase of the adventure.

You can always bank on an ex squaddie and an old friend when he greets you and the first words out of his mouth are "where the fuck have you been?" and "what took you so fucking long?" My response was immediate, I said "It's your fault, you fucking invited him!"

The way you can use the word 'fuck' in a variety of ways is typical for squaddies and their sense of humour, as it can be used in virtually any sentence with any amount of meanings. I am sure I've heard just about every form it can be used, during my 13 years army service and you do become desensitised to hearing it as it becomes a normal word that one would use in everyday language. It was as normal as using the word 'and' in a sentence.

We were indeed treated on our arrival. We were told to turn around and go back up the road as we were going to being filmed as we arrived. We also met a few of Ginge's German friends who greeted us well and had a quick chat. Because it was late and we had lots to do including dinner, we soon showered and changed ready for a late barbecue, a cold glass of well needed German beer, a quick catch up about the day's events and discussion on what we were going to do the following day before heading for bed around 01:00 am. It was a late one as Ginge put together the first part of the 'SOC's Tour to Istanbul' video that was to be uploaded to YouTube before we departed the following morning.

As soon as my head hit the pillow I was away in the land of nod, it seemed like a split second before the alarm clock was making that usual noise to inform me that I'd had enough sleep.

CHAPTER 4

Germany to Austria

Day 2 - Emsdetten to Kufstein (Germany to Austria)

Date: Wednesday 07 June 2017
Depart time: 06:00   **Arrive time:** 19:15

Days Mileage: 500 miles
Fuel cost: £36.30 approximately

Route:
Emsdetten (Germany) - Dortmund - Kassel - Würzburg - Munich - Kufstein (Austria)

Roads:
Motorway all the way, a brief ride through Munich and then A roads once near our destination.

Border crossing:
The Germany to Austrian border is an open border crossing, with no passport control.

Weather:
Raining, windy and cold to start with but brightened up in southern Germany. As we made our way towards Bavaria it became pleasant and improved as we finished the day.

Countries travelled & Currency:

	German	Euro	€
	Austria	Euro	€

The Days Events - The start of the adventure

T he alarm wasn't really needed as Ginge made enough noise to wake the dead, it was his first day after all, and he was just as excited to get going as we were yesterday. We were all up before 05:45 am, showered and changed ready for a very healthy breakfast along with a strong coffee, this would be copied for the rest of the trip (the coffee and not the healthy breakfast). Fruit, yogurt and a sprinkling of muesli filled a small gap as we'd eaten late the night before. The bikes were already packed from the previous evening so we were all ready pretty quickly.

Riding in Germany

Around 06:30 am bikes were ready to go, we started up and were heading off as the 'SOC's Tour' that had been in the planning for over a year. It was a quick start by Ginge as it was his first day. He took off like a rat out of an aqueduct! It didn't last very long though as we were soon into traffic and had to reduce the pace. The motorways were still pretty slow going in rush hour but only have two lanes and not three. All the same they were still moving better than ours do at this time in the morning. Ginge was soon at a respectable pace and slowed it down to a steady 85 mph, which is 130-140 kph on his German BMW R1200GS speedo.

Mike stuck himself at the back and very soon it became apparent he was being left behind. He really wasn't too happy at the higher speed and slowly drifted further back as we crunched up the miles. We continued at a steady pace as we had a long way to go and he would catch up regularly but had to really launch his bike to higher speeds, quite aggressively to get back in touch.

His lack of experience was showing early on but I had expected this to happen because of the previous day's ride to Germany. I was pretty sure he really didn't have any concept of big miles and had wanted frequent stops the day before. Riding big mileage isn't easy for everyone but you certainly cannot take a leisurely approach when you have big miles to do, as there are invariably problems to deal with - as we'd find out.

Mike was going to get tired very quickly playing catch up all the time, as dropping off and then having to ride faster to get back to the bikes ahead is extremely hard work and demanding. One of the reasons people find staying with bikes in front of them difficult, is because they listen to music and this interferes with their concentration levels as they get lost in the music they are listening to.

It is also a bit of a macho thing, not to be honest and say you are not experienced enough to ride in a certain way. Riders cannot maintain this kind of riding for prolonged periods of time, as it is exhausting. At this point in time we were not sure why he kept dropping off!

Bird strike at 110 mph

On one occasion, about half way down through Germany, Mike had dropped off so far that we couldn't see him, so we pulled over into a service station to find out what was wrong - was it him or his bike? He was trailing behind this time because he'd had a bird strike which had almost knocked him off the bike, broken the peak off his helmet, the visor had gone and the brand new Scala Radio comms system had snapped off and disappeared - suffice to say there is one less eagle flying around central Germany.

Mike reckoned his speed was in the region of at least 110 mph, as he was trying to close the gap between us when it happened. I'd seen the bird in question flying about 50 meters above us, when we'd passed the impact zone a few minutes earlier.

We pulled in and stopped at the next 'rastplatz' (German service station). A chap in a car said that our colleague had stopped on the hard shoulder further back. So we waited at the exit for Mike to show up. When he arrived we moved into the parking area for Mike to tell us about his experience. It was then that he commented that he was unhappy with the pace we were riding, as he couldn't keep up.

We explained that by dropping off and slowing down all the

time, it created a concertina effect and made the gaps very big. The problem is that it makes you have to ride much faster than those you are trying to catch up to and unfortunately this makes you much more fatigued, as you ride harder trying to catch up all the time. It also doesn't help when they are listening to music, it is a huge distraction and creates problems when riding in a group.

After that Ginge was quite happy to let me do the work to help Mike 'keep up to speed'. We were going to adopt a riding formation where each of us would ride in a certain position and have a role to play to help keep tighter together. I continued to try to help Mike throughout the tour, as he was definitely the weaker rider and probably not really up for this type of travelling on a motorcycle.

Hopefully though, the next 3 weeks of 'free advanced motorcycle training' would see him riding better in the future. After all riding at a steady 140 kph, is not very quick for an almost brand new GSA, time would tell!

He got a new dark visor put on his helmet and after a coffee and a quick chill out we were off again heading south. I tried to keep him in position but this was not an easy thing to do (in fact it was very difficult) and it just wasn't happening! He was reluctant to fit in to start with but eventually got into formation and found keeping together as rider number 2 easier, but losing concentration was his biggest fault and created problems for him.

Riding through central Germany

We headed south through the industrial belt of Dortmund, down towards Kassel on the Route 44 and then towards Würzburg on the Route 7, before picking up signs for Munich and then onto the Route 9.

The journey south towards Munich had some very difficult riding conditions at times, high wind, heavy rain and excessive spray from the road surface due to standing water. The road was carved out through and between huge forests. It was a beautiful sight to see and the open plains of crops and arable land was vast and unexpected, it was just like Spain for many miles as we rode south.

A real highlight was the hop farms, a smell very similar to cannabis (apparently) and I had been told that the German farmers in this area were the biggest hop growers in Europe. It really is an amazing country, clean and well presented with everything looking perfect and in its place.

BMW Motorrad Munich

We decided on a much needed detour for Mike. So we found the BMW dealership in Munich and headed into the city to sort out his broken helmet. We arrived before closing time and a welcome coffee break awaited us. I always thought the BMW dealership would give out free coffee to its customers but a nice little cafe inside the building was ready to relieve us of some money for their service.

Mike got his helmet sorted out before we headed south once again, where our next destination was Austria. Getting out of Munich took some time as we headed through the city centre for the most part, it was a beautiful city and somewhere I would like to visit at a later date to spend a few days and mooch about.

We were on our way again, on the autobahn heading straight for Austria. We were all tired and fatigued from a late night the evening before, an early start and the riding conditions were difficult because of the weather.

The sights en-route of the Alps were awesome and simply breathtaking. If it was the first time anyone had seen them, it would be a real treat and they'd end up slowing down and riding at a slower pace, so that they could take in every new view. I remembered them as a young soldier in the late 80's, seeing them for the first time, they were amazing then but even better now. I'm sure they are like a good bottle of port and get better with age, or is it that I appreciate views like this even more as I get older!

Open border going into Austria

The beautiful sights gave us a majestic entry into Austria. It was my first time over the border knowingly, but perhaps as a young squaddie climbing the mountains in those days, I may have inadvertently crossed the border whilst in Bavaria during my adventure training days. It was a long time ago, the memories fade with time but never really disappear. Seeing them again brought back a few pictures of long days walking the mountain passes and drunken nights having fun in Füssen.

Not long after crossing the border we arrived in Kufstein and checked into the Kufsteinerhof Hotel, it had been a long day. The speed was pretty slow for many parts of the journey and we could have been 'on it' (riding much quicker) for longer sections of the route. The hotel was pretty German looking, a kind of downstairs bar and restaurant area with a small reception. It looked very basic but very clean and tidy. All we wanted now was a hot shower, somewhere to dump our belongings and get sorted out.

We were shown our rooms, unloaded the bikes and carried our kit up a number of flights of stairs to the top floor. The rooms were all in a row and were big, spacious and very comfortable and would do the job for the evening. After showering I got a bit of personal downtime and headed outside to admire the views whilst waiting for the others to arrive. The place was just wonderful, overlooked by the Alps in the distance with magnificent views all around.

This was just the start of our adventures and I was like a kid in a sweet shop. For years I have looked after other people on tours around Europe and now I was getting to do this just for me. Don't get me wrong, I love touring with other people and holding their hand during their tentative first steps but this was a first for me and I felt totally free.

I was joined shortly afterwards by the others. We headed inside and grabbed a table to have a beer and order food. Whilst we were waiting we discussed the events of the day including Mike being attacked by a pterodactyl enroute.

We also collated all the SD cards and video footage onto Ginge's laptop whilst eating a large and well deserved dinner. We had another drink and as we felt tired from the swift 1,000 miles we'd ridden over the last two days, it wasn't not long before we headed off to bed.

CHAPTER 5

Austria

Day 3 - Kufstein to Villach via the GrossglocknerPass (Austria)

Date: Thursday 08 June 2017
Depart time: 08:00   **Arrive time:** 18:30

Days Mileage: 170 miles
Fuel cost: £16.95 approximately

Route:
Kufstein - Kitzbühel - Mittersill - GrossglocknerPass - Greifenburg - Villach - Faaker See (Lake)

Roads:
Fantastic A roads most of the way, slower mountain roads at the pass with breathtaking views. Finishing with a small section of motorway to end a long day.

Border crossing:
None

Weather:
Good, clear and sunny. Warmed up considerably after the Pass.

Countries travelled & Currency:

Austria   Euro   €

The Days Events - A spring in our steps

We were all up early, it had been a really comfortable night in a lovely town, but we hadn't been out and about because we had arrived late and it was only a stop over. If you want a tour where you are off out every night, sight seeing everywhere you visit, then this is definitely the wrong tour for you.

This was about going to Asia for Ginge and navigating '20 Countries in 20 Days' for me. Mike was just there for the adventure and experience, we all were really, but I'd made the '20 Countries in 20 Days' my mission for the trip, with a stop at Auschwitz towards the end as the icing on the cake.

Breakfast was the usual continental style, a selection of cold meats and cheeses, some boiled or scrambled eggs, cereal and of course a good few coffees to start the day. The night had gone quickly because we had all slept really well after the previous day's riding, and it had taken its toll on Mike and I from the two big days riding in poor weather conditions.

After we'd eaten, we headed to our rooms and packed our final bits and pieces. When we were ready to go, we filled up and got underway to travel through Austria on a famous pass. Because Ginge took more notice of his sat nav than the road signs, we ended up playing silly buggers trying to get out of Kufstein. After a bit of friendly banter, we finally headed out of town in the correct direction.

I hoped this was not going to be a taste of things to come, or I would have to change the name of the book to 'Three Ex-Trogs' (nickname given to RCT personnel by other Army units) and one sat nav.

Riding a motorbike in Austria

At the start of the journey over the pass we had to first negotiate the fast, open, long sweeping curves enroute to the 'Grossglockner Pass'. There were some great views, lovely villages and places that looked like they were out of a brochure, as we quietly made our way through many scenic places. The village buildings and houses looked very much like Bavarian properties but seemed more at home here in the Austrian mountain setting.

The roads and weather were nice as we went over the Pass. The going was very good as we hit the twisty roads and started to climb whilst we were en-route to the summit. The views were simply stunning and the riding was fast with Ginge leading the way.

Riding the Grossglockner Pass in Austria

On reaching the foot of the Grossglockner Pass, we were presented with a toll booth and relieved of €25.50 for the pleasure of riding over the mountain. We saw all kinds of cars and bikes, DB9's, Porsche's, sports cars, family cars, camper vans and hundreds of bikes, singular, in pairs, in groups, 125 autos, to the biggest Harley you can throw your leg over. After climbing many miles on good roads you could understand why there were so many people here, especially on a day when the weather was perfect for great views.

After travelling only half way up to the top of a fantastic ride towards the sky and where the climb was getting better and better with every turn, my BMW was not performing as it should. I got a stark reminder of how quickly and out of the blue things can suddenly go wrong, as I accelerated up the hill - No Power "shit", why now on the biggest Pass I'm ever likely to ride! The clutch was slipping, not that badly that I had to stop, but bad enough not to enjoy the roads. A mechanical failure can happen at any time, so I just concentrated on coaxing the bike to the top and not over revving as we continued to ascend.

Accelerating up the hill was fruitless, the bike had no guts, no drive to the back wheel, just noise and a slipping clutch. 'Fuck' was the first word that came to mind and as I eased back, the other two must have wondered what the hell I was doing so far back. I kept things to myself for some time, pondering over what options I had open to me but it is strange what thoughts wash through your mind at lightning speed.

Using breakdown recovery in Europe

Should I call the AA before things get worse, even though I

hadn't broken down yet? Should I limp to a local garage? Do I go to the next biggest BMW dealership and get 'raped without them giving me a reach around'. Or do I continue until I break down, pay for the repair, get car hire and continue? Or sack it right now and fly home, being reunited with the bike again weeks or months later! Decisions, decisions, decisions.

Ginge obviously knew something was wrong, so when he dropped back to enquire, I told him the news. "The clutch is fucked mate" was the answer he really didn't want to hear. I coaxed the bike to the top of the hill, it was hard getting one of those 'tractors' up to the top of the Pass fully laden and under 3,000 rpm. At the top we discussed my options. I didn't commit to anything, just talked it through and eased my way down the other side where there was hopefully going to be some big open twisty roads with not too many uphill routes to come.

Resigned to a £2000 bill or flying home I felt I was in a bit of a sticky situation, bail out now or bite the bullet. Either way the bike would have to be fixed somewhere and it was possibly going to be my last riding day. I started thinking I shouldn't have ridden it so hard in Portugal, but the bike had barely broken a sweat on its 2,500 mile test ride! Anyway, enough of what ifs, let's get to camp tonight and see how the land lies, was my only mission for the rest of the day.

Even with a few bike problems I still stopped for photos because that's the reason I came, for the adventure and the memories of where we were and where we'd been. We arrived at the top, more photo opportunities, videos and wow what awesome views we were presented with on such a clear day.

The ride up the Pass was an amazing journey, not a fast pace at all but very beautiful. The sheer scale of the mountains made me realise just how small and insignificant we really are. Looking back down onto the road below was exactly like the pictures in all the brochures - bends, curves, twists and turns as far as the eye could see and we'd just ridden up them.

The beauty at the top of the Grossglockner Pass

Once at the top we parked up and had a discussion about what the bike was doing and the possible outcomes. Before the trip had even started we were going to use the 'Top Gear Rules', break down and you are on your own! A little harsh you might think but when there is a definite goal in mind, like riding to Asia in a certain amount of time, you cannot get all sentimental about these things.

Mike headed off even further up the mountain to the very top, a journey I wasn't prepared to risk with my bike in its current state. It looked like a 1:1 from where we were stood and not many people were attempting it. Ginge and I had a chat and took a few photos, just admiring the views while mulling over a few more ideas.

I hadn't broken down yet so there was no point calling the AA to recover me, I reckoned I could coax the bike down the mountain as it was all downhill and as the sat navs on the BMW have a built in sitemap of all the BMW dealerships, we were in a pretty good position to know how far away different options were.

Mike came back and said that we should go up the hill to the top and see the views, he lent me his bike to go up and what a sight we were treated to. Ginge took the drone and we spent half an hour or so up there with the drone flying around as well as a few more happy snaps. Afterwards we headed back down to meet up with Mike and decided to take lunch before heading down the other side. Besides, if I did break down I didn't know when I'd be eating again.

A typical hearty lunch of 'currywurst mit pommes' washed down with a bottle of water, was enough to fill the gap. We had a chat with Mike to fill him in on the plans for the near future. Ginge had already made a comment to me while Mike was off on his own, that if I was going to get the bike fixed he was going to stay with me until it was repaired, because he didn't fancy heading off with Mike to complete the tour with just the two of them. He said that we'd just have to do motorways to make up any lost time. I thought this was a very nice gesture being as the 'Top Gear Rules' were high on his agenda before the trip commenced, but I understood what was being said and I didn't need it spelling out!

There were loads of idiots on the Pass who thought they could ride, showing off, peer pressure, group spirits running high - you could see why so many bikers get killed or have serious injuries. Actual ability versus perceived ability, most of these idiots were crap and that was being polite! We overtook some clowns who thought they were good, their riding was extremely poor, their planning even worse. I stayed in 3rd and 4th gear using my brakes to slow down instead of using the engine as I wanted to limit the amount of acceleration and clutch wear.

These idiots would ride fast in all the straights but drop to walking speed in the corners. We had descended a fair way down when we had to stop at temporary traffic lights where the road was being repaired. They overtook us so that they were in front again - even though we'd overtaken them in the corners beforehand, sheer idiots who needed lots of training, we'll soon pass you again my friends was my inner thought.

A second opinion

When we eventually got down to the bottom of the mountain and onto the flatter lowlands, Ginge wanted to have a ride on my bike to see what he thought. He'd had the same model bike before for a number of years so knew exactly how it should feel and ride, so once off the pass Ginge took the tractor (BMW) for a brief ride. We stopped in a rest area where there was a little cafe. Ginge said "It's fucked, it won't last a week". "Yes I know, I'm lucky to be here and not stuck up the mountain". We had a laugh and joke, it's funny how you can turn any problem into a story and take the piss at the same time.

Yes I thought, I was homeward bound and out of the tour early, or a few grand lighter with the possibility of meeting up 4-6 days later having to wait for a repair. At least Carolyn (my future ex-wife) would be happy with me not making it to Asia! But the remark by Ginge about not leaving me with the 'Top Gear Rules' and staying together gave me a slightly different take on the situation.

The bike would have to be repaired somewhere, so why not in Austria or Slovenia, if I made it that far, besides this was only Day 3. I would be happy to go home now because so far I'd had a cracking time but really it had only just started. What was the point of flying home, getting the bike recovered and then in a few weeks or months time being reacquainted with the bike and getting it repaired by a local garage!

After thrashing a new GS for a few miles, I had to give Ginge his bike back. He didn't want to ride my old failing 'tractor' for any longer than he had to. That was it - decision made, I would ride it until it broke down and then get recovered to a garage to repair it, that was my plan - for now.

Seeking advice and help

So, while we were waiting for our coffee to be served at a lovely spot where the cafe overlooked a beautiful blue/green lake with stunning views around, I had a brain wave to call one of the bike shops/mechanics I know. They were bound to give me some sound advice. First of all I tried Simon Fear at Arden Motorcycles in Alcester, where I'd purchased the bike. Failing a conversation with him I could call Doug Ashbourne at Doug's Cycles in Studley as he'd offered his help if I needed it.

I called and Simon answered the phone. He asked what was wrong with a few questions, as he needed more information for giving any possible solutions. It had run well enough for the trip to Portugal and had no previous signs of the clutch slipping, so in my mind there could possibly be an alternative answer or fix. Simon at Arden was on the ball, I told him the fault and what was happening and he relayed what possible issues and problems it could be. We discussed common faults and what work had been done to the bike prior to going away.

His advice was to remove some fluid from the clutch reservoir and make sure the fluid was not touching the diaphragm. Secondly check for any leaks at the bleed nipple, then to check the adjustment on the lever and make sure the hand guards were not fowling the lever. Sometimes this prevents the clutch from releasing properly.

With all of the above checked, it was time for a test ride. All ready and eager to see what was going to happen we set off. Gently to start with and then steadily getting braver with the power, then the horns came out - in for a penny, in for a pound and as Neil Bolton from NB Services would say, the bike had to 'have it' - and it did. As I disappeared into the distance with Ginge in tow it was very, very apparent that one or all of the solutions had indeed fixed the bike!

Well done Simon from Arden Motorcycles for his knowledge and experience - just the job. The saying goes 'it's not what you know, it's who you know' and it was very true now. The moral of the story is never hang your jacket on the handlebar, it may dislodge the hand guard and engage the clutch lever! This was certainly rider error - a huge lesson that would not be repeated.

How not to ride an R6

So, with the bike sorted on the long twisty open fast roads afterwards, we left an R6 spinning at the side of the road as we overtook him, he was solo and we were fully laden. Ginge and I sniggered as we saw him getting smaller and smaller in our mirrors, after he'd given chase and tried to keep up with us.

The roads were open, sweeping and amazing all the way to Villach. We stopped once for a thumbs up to make sure I was back on track and we were like the three musketeers as we rode on. We decided to stop at an Aldi supermarket for food and wine for an evening by the lake.

We arrived at the lake side in 'Faaker See' in good time and checked in, to pay our camping fee. It was still light and warm which gave us enough time to pitch the tents and get ourselves sorted out and have a dip in the lake to cool down after a long hot and sweaty day.

We had a quick bite to eat and headed for the on site bar for a well deserved and celebratory beer before heading to bed for a much needed rest and good night's sleep. It was a bad night for me, cold, freezing cold and I was dithering for the most part, even waking up during the night to put a few more layers on.

I needed a blanket or a second doss bag to keep me warm, in my old age I'd got a bit soft and I like to be kept in the manner I've become accustomed to. We certainly didn't live the high life on these tours and as Bilbo Baggins said "I'm too old for adventures!".

CHAPTER 6

Austria to Slovenia

Day 4 - Faaker See to Sežana
(Austria to Slovenia)

Date: Friday 09 June 2017
Depart time: 10:00   **Arrive time:** 19:15

Days Mileage: 140 miles
Fuel cost: £15.21 approximately

Route:
Faaker See (Austria) - Podkoren (Slovenia) - Jesenice - Lake Bled - Podbrdo - Tolmin - Ajdovščina - Štorje - Sežana

Roads:
Some brilliant A roads to more intricate B roads. What a fabulous day in the northern Slovenia National Park. Great views and scenery, a real treat that we weren't expecting.

Border crossing:
Austria to Slovenia - No passport control in place. There is a border area with disused buildings that are not manned for stopping vehicles in transit as you pass through the border

Weather:
Weather was getting hotter, now down to a t shirt under the textiles. We have been wearing base layers up to now.

Countries travelled & Currency:

	Austria	Euro	€
	Slovenia	Euro	€

The Days Events - A cold start

An early start was definitely on the cards today to warm up. I'd had very little sleep as it was freezing cold during the night, or at least it was in my £10 doss bag (sleeping bag) from

Aldi! Oh, how I wish I'd brought a much better sleeping bag with me, or found a blanket to purchase last night when we stopped for food. I must have had a maximum of 2 hours sleep tops, so I suppose I was feeling a little bit sorry for myself. I knew Bilbo Baggins was right, I am definitely too old for these type of adventures - long days and sleepless nights are not going to see me through this tour, that's for sure!

I woke up very early but didn't get up until 06.30 am. Still freezing cold, I begged some hot water from Ginge for a cup of hot lemon to start the warming up process. I then headed off to the shower block for a boiling hot shower to warm up, as the hot lemon hadn't lasted very long and hadn't done the trick. After a fabulous hot shower, I was warm, awake and ready to start the day with a bit of breakfast and looking forward to the rest of the day.

A very lucky chance meeting

When the cafe opened the plan was to have a quick coffee and be on our way early but this didn't happen because into the campsite rode two Slovenia registered bikes, these two guys greeted us as friends and enquired about our travels. We told them where we were heading and politely asked about theirs. Our day was about to be drastically changed and be turned completely on its head.

A late start had definitely not been planned. Mike was leading the route, as per our initial brief and planning stage back in Tenbury Wells in April. Unfortunately he had not done any routes in the months leading up to the tour, so in true army fashion he was going to cuff-it (do an ad hoc version that is hopefully successful). At that very moment, his luck changed as the two riders were Balkan Tour guides from Alkemist Adventures running their own business. They gave us a route and places to see along the way, what luck that was, eh Mike!

They were very well spoken chaps, just off to Germany to finalise a deal with Touratech for their Baltic Tour guide company. "Any tips guys" was the phrase Mike used as he hadn't planned any of his routes as agreed, whilst he was back in the UK. This was like a penny from heaven, his luck was about to change big time.

They got the map out straight away and pointed out where the best places were and how to get there, they gave detailed advice on other areas to ride to and what we should be careful of. They also told us about riding in Albania and Croatia, which would be a great source of information for us to use at a later date. We were guided into a National Park where very few bikers venture because there are small 'B' roads and perhaps don't look too interesting but being as these guys knew the area well, we were not about to simply ignore their advice. They also recommended a place to stop on the evening, a small village with fantastic local wines, we were well up for a bit of that after a long day in the saddle riding.

So with a route now planned, it changed the day completely, a coffee or two and 2 hours later (while Mike hastily plotted a route into his sat nav) we were off.

Riding out of Austria

We said our goodbyes after exchanging business cards and went in search of fuel ready for the day ahead. This is because we'd been told about some twisty roads and a few new passes to explore and there probably wasn't going to be a garage. After filling up we left the area of Faaker See.

The roads were great, even better than the previous day and we soon arrived at the border as it was only about 10-12 kms away. We got the all important pictures and videos done, especially for Ginge as he wanted to get the Union flag out in every new country and Continent as a reminder to his future offspring that he and his family are well travelled.

It is a brilliant idea, as he has his family tree embroidered on the union flag and adds every country where the family has been and flown the flag.

Riding a motorbike in Slovenia

After a hassle free border crossing that seemed desolate and disused we headed up one of the passes and the views were absolutely stunning. It wasn't the Grossglockner but it was truly awesome to ride up, but unfortunately somewhere high on the peak the Trenta Pass was closed. We were told by a guy fixing the road and by some bikers who were returning from getting as far as they could but had had to return. We didn't know why the pass was closed but the red line through the name of the next town on the sign post soon became apparent, that's what they do in this country for a road closure to a certain destination.

So, the Trenta Pass the Tour Guides had told us to ride over was closed. The way up there had looked promising and we were not at all disappointed with the views, but now a slight problem, a detour would not be an easy one because of the lie of the land. Have you ever tried to ride around a mountain? They are huge in Slovenia, this was going to be one hell of a de-tour. There wasn't another way to go and the 206 (road number) was the only road over the mountain, unless we ventured east and travelled through Italy to drop south again. We decided to KBO (Keep Buggering On - a famous Winston Churchill saying) and head to Lake Bled which was on our previous agenda but It was going to turn into a long day. This is because we had to backtrack and then head in the totally wrong direction to where we'd been told to go. Still Lake Bled was supposed to be a fab place to visit and our new plans diverted us away from the mountain pass.

A de-tour was okay because the roads were just fabulous to ride, open, twisty stuff, a marvellous view around every corner, beautiful and outstanding all at the same time. We were all gobsmacked by the roads and scenery, we were truly in love with this beautiful country.

The Beauty of Lake Bled

We had lunch not far from Lake Bled at a small but lovely little restaurant where we learnt how to say please, thank you and how to ask for the bill. We'd found a little pizza place in the middle of nowhere (well it wasn't lost, so it didn't need finding) but we'd stumbled upon it after Mike got himself geographically challenged (lost). The service, the waitress and the food were all 5 star, we were well attended to and looked after. A few new phrases were written down for future reference and we asked for the bill with our new found language skills and were happy with the small price for such a great lunch. We'd only eaten half a pizza each at the most because they were so big.

Ginge chatted to a local biker while we paid up, who informed him that we MUST do the Croatian coast road. The whole way, no diversion inland, just the whole way because it was reported that it was 1,100 kms long and something that you had to do. In fact the guy told Ginge he was 'fucking stupid' for not riding the best coast road in the world, as our original route would have been to Zagreb.

A quick refuel for our bodies, a bit of sightseeing done (at the female cyclists who changed their tops whilst in the restaurant) and then we were off to Lake Bled and beyond. Arriving at Lake Bled, we could see why it was so popular, with its stunning views and places of interest dotted around the lake. Ginge stood up most of the time, not sure if it was because his arse was sore/numb, if he was practicing his twerking or he was trying to 'letch' at the bikini clad bathers around the lake. The crystal clear blue waters obviously attracted this type of nonsense but we were far too busy discovering new places on our journey, so we pushed on with Mike at the helm.

Then the treat really started. As we left Bled the roads and views over the national park got bigger and better. Very few vehicles and even less bikes - our personal Slovenian tour guides had not disappointed us, with fast sweeping roads, tight twisty roads, uphill hairpins, downhill open curves, closed views, open views, beautiful views and much more.

We rode big 'A' roads along with single track lanes barely big enough for cars, but the thing that really set it apart were the roads to die for and the views that we were seeing (usually only seen in brochures). Everywhere we stopped people wanted to talk or ask if we needed help. Cars would stop, people even turned round and came back to offer advice on how to reach destinations.

Stunning Slovenia

The scenery was just breathtaking, one of the best roads that I'd ever ridden, with views to match. WOW, WOW and WOW these words don't do it any justice at all. Miles and miles of twisty roads in valley floors, with greenery and forests either side. Gorges lined with mountains either side, with views just like in a brochures to lure you there. A winding road in the middle of 2-3 km flat plains, flanked by huge mountains, and then forests like you've never seen before. The Black Forest and Sherwood Forest are mere copses in comparison. High in the hills and mountains were beautiful houses set into the side of the land-scape with tremendous views, what a lovely place this was.

The open gorges with flat valley floors for at least 2 miles were lined with more mountains, while the road meandered like a river down the middle of the channel, peaks and passes, hairpins and 'S' bends, this country had it all. The nature reserves were places of beauty, they did not let this place down at all. We were certainly off the beaten track and saw very few bikers, was this luck or a very direct result of the tour guides? Whichever it was it contributed to a memorable day. Mike said that yesterday was the best days riding he'd ever done but today he changed his mind. This was certainly a day to remember.

Everywhere we went, people in general, locals, tourists and other bikers were pleased to meet us and wanted to discuss routes, roads and our start and destination point, not because they were nosey but because they were genuinely interested. We were blown away by how welcome we felt and by how we were received in this beautiful little country.

We were getting tired after the previous long cold night with little sleep, so we pushed on. A Hungarian couple stopped at the petrol station where we were filling up, and we exchanged stories of adventure and we were told that we must visit Budapest on our journey north after Asia. So it's in our notes to look at it closer to the time.

The sat nav didn't disappoint either, they are a pain in the arse! Mike got to a junction, he started dithering over his sat nav and after a few fumbling seconds made his decision. He only had to choose left or right, he chose to turn right which meant the river was on our left!

I knew when we were heading the wrong way, as I was map reading and had a good idea of the area from having the map on my tank bag. The river should definitely be on our right hand side for us to be going to the right way but as usual the sat nav had other plans. It adds more miles to the journey so that we value its worth, perhaps it gets lonely sat in its overnight cover when we finish riding or it wants to be more involved and extend its part in the days ride.

Well not tonight I thought, the sat nav is not taking us on a wild goose chase, time was getting on and I did not want a late finish. I overtook and stopped Mike and insisted the sat nav was wrong, yet again! Would these words 'come back to haunt me' later on? So I took the lead and went the right way, all the way to our next destination of Dutovlje.

At what we thought was our final destination we stopped for

a well needed drink and to have a break. Out came the booking.com app on the phone and we found out there wasn't any accommodation in the area that could look after our needs, so we headed for the nearest biggest place as they were bound to have something available for us just for the night.

Near the Italian Border

Another 10 miles or so and we were in Sežana. We found a hotel on the phone app and decided to just turn up and chance it, after all we were right by the Italian border and there was a coast not far away. Who in their right minds would be stopping here if you had a coast venue to choose from. When we arrived the hotel staff were very helpful but they couldn't give us the rooms we required as they were fully booked, it looked like they had some sort of event going on and they were very busy. It was a boutique style hotel, olde worlde and very plush, but they called another nearby hotel for us and reserved three rooms.

We were given directions and headed off as it was now getting on a bit, much later than planned. Detours, diversions, road closures and missed turns had all added to the delay but we were in one piece and happy to be heading to a hotel with a comfy bed and a hot shower. We arrived at Hotel Safir which was also a casino, this was going to be base for the night, later than planned but we were in good spirits after a fantastic days riding.

A small beer on arrival, a shower and relax for an hour and then dinner with a glass of wine, recommended by our tour guides earlier this morning finished off a marvellous day. After the meal we were all ready for an early night, without too much chat and going over the day's events. I'd had enough to drink with a beer and a wine and I was ready for a good night's sleep. Personally this was my best day on the bike that I'd had to date. Whether it was luck or good judgement I'll never know but big smiles all round and Slovenia is a must for any biker, but you must get off the beaten track and you will definitely have a well rewarded treat.

We were less than 1km from the Italian border, it would be 'rude' not to nip over and add another country to the trips tally in the morning, wouldn't it?

CHAPTER 7

Slovenia to Croatia

Day 5 - Sežana to Starigrad
(Slovenia to Croatia)

Date: Saturday 10 June 2017
Depart time: 09:00   **Arrive time:** 16:30

Days Mileage: 170 miles
Fuel cost: £16.02 approximately

Route:
Sežana (Slovenia) - Fernetti (Italy) - Kozina (Slovenia) - Jelovice (Croatia) - Podgorje - Vodice - Rijeka - Senj - Starigrad

Roads:
Motorway to begin with and then went inland on some small country lanes, went south into Croatia and they turned onto the best coast road I have ever ridden.

Border crossing:
Going from Slovenia to Croatia there was a border control entering Croatia, the border guards wanted to see passports and bike documents.

Weather:
Hot and mostly sunny, up to 30 degrees.

Countries travelled & Currency:

	Slovenia	Euro	€
	Italy	Euro	€
	Croatia	Kuna	kn

The Days Events - An unfriendly start

As soon as my head hit the pillow I was out like a light. I had a bottle of water for during the night but hadn't woken up at all, so it was still full and I was still in the same position as when I'd fallen asleep. A good night's sleep, I was fully recharged and ready to go. I headed to breakfast and met up with the others at about 08:00 am, it was the usual continental style, with a hot plate and buffet style set up. It was hearty with some nice strong coffee to wash it down, that would keep us awake for a good few hours. After breakfast we were ready to check out at around 09:00 am.

I must admit we were met with an unfriendly welcome at breakfast and had enjoyed the same frosty reception the previous evening too. The hotel was very good, it was clean and comfortable but the service was very poor. We didn't mind as we were only using it as a quick stop over to sleep, recharge ourselves and our batteries for the electrical devices. We would only be there less than 12 hours, most of which would be in bed sleeping and we'd be off again as soon as we were ready, so didn't give the place a second thought as we would never be returning anyway, 'any port in a storm' as they say.

A quick ride into Italy

After breakfast we loaded up and departed. As the Italian border was so close we decided to head over there for a happy snap and add another country to our tally. We didn't really ride into any specific part of Italy, just through the border crossing to say we'd been there, and as it was an open border it was easy to go in and turn around (we took the necessary photos to prove it). After visiting Italy we headed straight on the toll road to get out of Sežana. It was a difficult place to navigate really, as the roads were pretty badly signposted and there were lots of little turnings, and we just wanted to get going and head to the Croatian border, as we didn't want to keep having long days in the saddle.

We'd agreed the previous night that it was my turn to lead, so I obliged and planned the route on a route card. During the day I was going to half use the sat nav (I hate the things with a passion) but have succumbed to using one as an aid to the map. I had toll roads and motorways programmed into the sat nav, I wanted the quickest way to the road we needed. This was because of the detour last night as we were quite a way off track, according to our original plan.

Enroute the typical thing happened on the sat nav, it said turn off at the next junction. As soon as we were off the road, it was telling me to go back on the main road - WTF! As we did, it told me to turn around when possible. I ignored it and carried on for it to recalculate, it did and brought us off at the next junction, as soon as we were off it froze - my language is not describable at this stage.

Instead of playing with the sat nav, I got my mobile phone out. I got the mobile data working and found out our location. Did a bit of map reading from google maps and got straight onto a back road that would take us straight into Croatia. We were now on a small side road that was empty, the views weren't great because of the trees but we were making good progress.

The Croatian border on a motorbike

It wasn't too long before we reached the Croatian border. The guard took our passports and bike documents and we made friendly chit chat with him and before long our passports were returned. Next was to take a few happy snaps with Ginge and the Union Flag, he had already positioned himself with the Croatian flag and border guard in the background for the shot. This was going to be our daily routine from now on as Ginge hadn't crossed many of these borders before. After we'd taken advantage of the remote border post it wasn't long before we were riding again into the woodlands of the northern part of the country and the Croatian border was slowly getting further away.

The weather was hotting up and so were the roads. The villages were virtually derelict and the roads were in some need of repair and lots of attention but we were in a new country and looking forward to seeing what Croatia had to offer.

Villages were run down and Mike reckoned it was from the ethnic cleansing back in the 1990's. I was not well read on this but I was based here as a soldier and didn't really understand the full history and reasons behind the war. I felt a bit embarrassed by not knowing but I intended to study about it. Especially because I was thinking of returning at a later date, when I bring an organised tour here. It was naive of me to have been here during that period and not to know what it was all about and any of its history. Maybe I had been told but had forgotten, it wasn't really a good enough excuse for my ignorance though!

The roads started getting better the further south we went, from a small 'B' road to an 'A' road and we were soon onto good tarmac again. It wasn't long before we were on the coast road and heading for a town. Where was this fantastic road? I thought as we headed into Rijeka. We had obviously come from inland into the town as we dropped down the hill towards the waterfront and a very pretty looking harbour.

We'd done about 150 miles so we decided to fill up, have a coffee at the harbour and watch a yacht race start. We got talking to a guy from London, who was on business and he was gobsmacked by our story. We enjoyed half an hour or so with him as we chatted and passed a bit of time enjoying the view.

We were soon on our way once more. Having a pitstop is really important as it gives you time to relax and refresh before setting off again. Our normal routine was to stop every 150-200 miles for fuel and pitstop for us to take on food and water, but after we set off and headed south again the most amazing thing happened. OMG (Oh My God) within 10 miles or so of us leaving we were on what can only be described as absolutely the best biking road in the world.

This road had it all, the amount of bikers enjoying it was insane, the traffic was light and we were having the time of our lives. Long twisty stuff, bend after bend after bend, banking left to right for mile after mile after mile, in fact from one fuel stop to the next!

Riding a motorcycle in Croatia

Yet again, this road was just perfect. The only bikes that passed us were solo sports bikes that were unladen. Now and again a lone rider would pass in shorts and a t-shirt, but every single one acknowledged each other as friends - what a place. We had the coast on our right hand side. It would stay there for the next thousand kilometres or so and it was truly breathtaking and unexplainable by its sheer beauty.

You could stop every hundred meters for a new photo opportunity but the journey would take far too long. We rationed ourselves to a few pictures now and again, as we would be there for weeks if we decided to stop for every wonderful view that we came across.

We headed south for Senj as that was the next largest town. There was really no need to map read as it was just a case of following the coast road all the time. It got to around 1:00 pm and we decided it was time to feed ourselves. There were lots of places to stop and we had some lunch in a beautiful, idyllic restaurant in a little cove overlooking a bay with a few boats and people enjoying the sun. There were no sandy beaches, just rocks and pebbles, but the rocks were flat and pretty comfortable with sun beds and the sea was a turquoise blue like you only see in the 'touched up' brochures. The sights were just staggering and we were so happy to be enjoying the road, the country, the company and the fact that we were there. The road was that good we just wanted to get back on it.

After lunch the roads didn't change at all, bends, bends and more bends and lots of them. Toes scraping on the ground on either side as the roads followed the contours of the mountains, anywhere from 5-500 meters from the Adriatic Sea on our right hand side. The sea was crystal clear and deep blue (in the deeper places) and looked so inviting for a dip later on. The islands off the coast changed the landscape all the time and we did not get sick of the tremendous views at all.

Perfect riding in Croatia

Absolutely fabulous I thought, just what the doctor ordered at this time in my life, as I was transitioning through a fairly tough and stressful period. I must admit I was delighted to have said yes to this amazing tour. The riding was just outstanding and I had a newfound love for my own personal motorcycling. This was a long tour and I was well aware that the bike could not be ridden hard for the whole duration but for now, I was going to really enjoy the roads. The bike and I deserved that after almost an early exit when I thought the clutch was on it's way out. Oh, and did I enjoy those roads - it would not be the last time I ventured down them, that's for certain.

Birthday celebrations

Today was also Ginge's birthday, so we spoilt him and let him decide on a place to stay that evening. He could have chosen anywhere but after he'd had enough fun for one day, he started looking for a place to pull over. We pulled in, it wasn't wild camping but a large village called Starigrad on the coast.

We found a room by chance, that was inexpensive. They were pondering over having us for just one night, but in fact we wouldn't even be there for 12 hours and they were eventually happy to accept €90 from us for the evening. Three separate double rooms, that were basic, spacious, very clean and tidy. We gave them our passports, paid up and took our stuff off the bikes to take to our rooms.

We gave Ginge the SD cards and video footage of the day and he stayed in his room to transfer the stuff onto his laptop. The reason he did it was because Mike and I wanted to go for a late afternoon dip in the sea and Ginge wasn't really into sunbathing or sitting in the sun. No wondered with a nickname like his!

After our dip we headed to a local bar for a quick beer before bumping into two Croatian lads who have obviously been on the beer all afternoon. We had a good natter with them and they insisted we had a proper Croatian beer from their plastic carrier bag. It was very warm and not very nice at all but we went along with their hospitality and they told us about the best roads to go on for the rest of our trip in Croatia. After a short while we made our excuses and headed back to shower and meet up with the 'Birthday Boy'.

We found out the name of a decent restaurant on the seafront and after getting ready, headed down to the coast with the drone. We made time in the early evening to get some drone footage, but Ginge accidentally knocked his sunglasses into the water. It was a good job that he was fluent in German as there was a German family on holiday and it just so happened that their son had a small fishing net. He was able to retrieve the glasses with some careful netting, otherwise Ginge would have been wet going to fish them out of the 4 foot deep boat mooring area.

After our brief conversation and gratitude we wandered off for dinner. It was a great location and a really nice meal, with a glass or two of very cold white wine to wash down my perfectly grilled sea bream. It had been a fabulous way to finish a great day, we'd had a good laugh and were once again looking forward to a good night's sleep as tomorrow promised to be just as good as today. What a treat we'd have if it was, we certainly couldn't wait.

CHAPTER 8

Croatia

Day 6 - Starigrad to Dubrovnik (Croatia)

Date: Sunday 11 June 2017
Depart time: 08:00   **Arrive time:** 16.30

Days Mileage: 240 miles
Fuel cost: £35.16 approximately

Route:
Starigrad (Croatia) - Zadar - Šibenik - Split - Ploče - Neum (Bosnia and Herzegovina) - Dubrovnik (Croatia)

Roads:
This is said to be the best coastal road in the world, I personally think it is one of the best you will find. It's a long and brilliant road, with bend after bend, curve after curve and beautiful views for the duration. I will definitely be back here for a ride on this road!

Border crossing & Insurance:
Croatia to the Bosnia and Herzegovina border was a lengthy process, it seemed a little bit chaotic. When we arrived at the front of the queue, the border guard looked at our passports only and waved us through.

Bosnia and Herzegovina to Croatia a few miles away was a simple process, it was much quicker as we showed passports and were let back into Croatia.

I was not insured in Bosnia and Herzegovina. We weren't told to purchase any insurance at the border and besides were only travelling a very short distance along the coast (5.7 miles), we didn't bother to enquire about buying any either.

Weather:
Very hot and sunny 36+ degrees with clear blue sky.

Countries travelled & Currency:

	Croatia	Kuna	kn
	Bosnia & Herzegovina	Convertible mark	km

The Days Events - Up early and ready to go

W e were all early risers, some earlier than others, so we decided to just get up and go once we were ready. Mike was usually up first, followed by me at about 06:00 am and then Ginge, who thought that early rising was waking up with morning glory! No alarm clocks were needed as we were keen to be on our way today and that edge of excitement ensured we didn't over sleep. The weather was absolutely fabulous at that time in the morning, 06:00 am in a holiday place near the coast was a very peaceful time, that was until we got up and then all hell broke loose.

On waking up and chatting, we'd all had a pretty rough night's sleep. Ginge was up between 8-10 times in the night hunting down mosquitos. His wall was splattered with patches of blood as a reminder to next B&B visitors that keeping their windows shut was the best way to keep out the mozzies, or that they should buy a plug in mosquito killer! Mike had a few bites and said that he'd been disturbed too. Not by Ginge hammering on the walls but by the little annoying things that always seem to buzz in your ear and scare you half to death in the night, as you frantically wave your hands about in the dark trying to get rid of that awful buzzing sound.

I didn't get off scot free and had several bites and a number of wide awake moments in the night too. My defence was to make a makeshift tent in the bed with the sheet over the headboard but that only seemed to trap the little blighters in the gap and there seemed to be more than there really were. The last time I heard mozzies like this I was sleeping rough in the Army 30 years ago in a hot humid German forest, in the middle of no-where playing Army.

We were packed up, loaded the bikes and were ready to head off around 07:00 am. We weren't that quiet and I think we must have disturbed most of the neighbours. One old lady came to speak to us and as she only spoke German as her second language, Ginge spoke to her. He discussed where we came from and where we were going. She was a chatty old lady and seemed to have a good sense of humour with lots of smiles and laughter. I could only make out bits of the conversation as I hadn't listened to any German language since living there in the 1980's. She wished us good luck and her final words were 'if you make it!". We weren't sure if she meant because we were bikers or because we were going to Istanbul, but we kind of laughed it off as we prepared to leave.

Searching for breakfast

We headed out onto the road to fill up before we left the village. There was a cafe next door so we stopped for a coffee and some toast but were told "sorry no food"! So we just had coffee and went on our way again and not before too long (around 70 miles later), we stopped at another cafe/grill and were told exactly the same again, "no food". Do these people not eat anything in the morning, we enquired to each other. Nope, it appears not, as they all sit there with a coffee or some other drink and nothing else. We didn't stop and were off again to find some food. 75 miles later we stopped again, this time in Split and Ginge put "fast food" into his sat nav. Up popped 'McDonald's' cheers Ginge - more crap to keep us going, "I'd rather eat cardboard" I said.

As we headed towards McDonald's we saw a place that said 'fast food,' it looked open, so we made a U-Turn and stopped. Sorry, they said, no food until lunchtime, it was 10:30 am now so we had to make a decision. If we were quick we'd make McDonald's for breakfast or we could continue on our journey still hungry. Food was needed as we were starting to feel a bit jaded from the heat. We needed a stop and some food to keep up our concentration on these types of fast twisty roads. Following the sat nav took us to a shopping mall, WTF? But as it happened there was a large food hall inside, so we didn't end up eating crap after all. We needed fuel for our bodies, as did the bikes, to continue the journey. The roads had started to get better and it was getting hotter by the minute.

Today was a pretty big day, 350 kms to ride and if the roads were like yesterday's we'd be in for a treat. From leaving, the roads were initially okay, not up to the same standard as the previous day at all, but once we had cleared Split they started to open up, fast sweeping things to tight hairpins, as they once again followed the mountain contours. The views were spectacular and the beauty of this place was really special to see. Have I sold you the idea of a trip to Croatia yet? They were amazingly good and getting better all the time. Holidaymakers miss all of this when they are stuck on the beach all day, but don't tell everyone about this road, it needs to be kept a bikers secret!

I thought Ginge was behind me as we continued but it was a guy leading a group from Austria. He looked the same frame as Ginge and on the same bike. Oops, I'd got a wriggle on and hadn't seen Mike or Ginge for some time. I stopped for another tank of fuel and got a call from Mike, they weren't that far back. They thought I'd turned off and gone to another small place on the coast, with a similar name to where I wanted to stop off. I told them I was well ahead of them and waited for them to catch up. They arrived within 10 minutes or so and filled up with fuel and we took the time to enjoy an ice-cream and a cold bottle of water.

Bringing back memories

We rode the short distance of 80 miles towards Ploče from Split, this journey had taken 2 hours or so in a truck many years before. We were going to make a special stop in Ploče, which was where I had lived for 6 months during the conflict in the early 90's when serving in the Army. The reason we were based there was because it was a natural harbour and our vehicles were transported to there by ship. We had set up a camp in this location to act as United Nations. Our units were quite unique as we didn't have white vehicles like the UN used. Our vehicles were green and camouflaged for a different reason. If the 'shit hit the fan' we could quickly discard our blue beret and turn into an aggressive force, to help sort out the issues that were going on there at the time. The unit was 24 Airmobile Brigade based in Colchester in its normal peacetime role.

I didn't recognise anywhere en-route as the signs had been removed when we were there. The places had grown into tourist attractions (and rightly so) but I did remember one or two of the mountain views as the road elevated up to 300 meters above sea level in certain places. When we turned inland just before Ploče there was no doubt where I was. The memories came flooding back and I recalled being back there 25 years earlier.

I was able to ride straight to where I had lived all those years ago. To the exact same hanger, next to the sea, where we called home in the early days, before moving to the flattened reclaimed marshland, that the Engineers had transformed into a 'tent city'.

The hanger was exactly the same but was full of stores instead of squaddies. It was now a ferry port too, where you had to go through a gated barrier to get into the dock area. We managed to ride around the barrier to get access as there was nobody about. Across the harbour was the old church and houses that I used to wake up to every morning against the backdrop of hills.

We didn't really have the time to go off wandering around the whole area but I was glad I'd taken the time to visit this distant memory location. It had good and bad memories for me, and once the nostalgic pictures had been taken I was happy to get back on the road and away from there.

We headed out a slightly different way to the way we'd come in, we were soon on the road south heading once again in the direction of Dubrovnik. The roads were still very good and enjoyably fast and twisty. Just before we got to the border we stopped next to what looked like a beautiful lake but was actually the sea. There were many stalls selling local produce at the side of the road. They were selling all sorts of fruit and drinks. When we used to drive around here during the conflict we would buy wine by the litre and fill up anything we had, as they decanted wine from large barrels. Now they were a bit more up to date and sold wine by the bottle, so Mike purchased some after he'd heard my story.

Another Border Crossing

The border crossing into Bosnia and Herzegovina was quite a long process. Would we need to purchase motorcycle insurance to transit through the short time we were passing through the country and were they going to insist on seeing all our documents?

The border was a little congested. We were in a line next to a dozen Austrian riders. I asked where they were going and they responded "To the best roads in Europe." They were going to Montenegro for 5 days and insisted that the roads there were ten times better than Austria, which I found an odd statement, as the roads in Austria and Slovenia seemed pretty special to me. Once we said our goodbyes we were next in line at the border crossing. As they saw our UK passports they waved us straight through. The Bosnian road was very good too as the landscape mirrored Croatia. Not unusual really, I don't know why we expected anything different as this was the former Yugoslavia and the coastal scenery was exactly the same.

We made pretty good time through the 6 miles in Bosnia and were soon back in Croatia, but not before the union flag picture and traditional stop that we enjoyed with every new country. We knew this was going to be a 'country ritual' so it became a bit of fun and we got on with the proceedings. We were soon underway again and in the blink of an eye were back at the Croatian border and heading towards Dubrovnik.

A German motorbike passed us with a female pillion passenger, two side panniers and the passenger was loaded down with a pretty large rucksack. This chap could ride! We tagged on behind him and it was one of the most pleasurable rides so far for me. It was a very fast pace, twisty roads, good overtakes and a real pleasure to watch and be part of. It got the adrenalin pumping and brought a huge smile to my face as I grinned all the way to Dubrovnik.

If he made an overtake and there was a blind bend ahead for me not to pass, he would gesture that it was okay with a thumbs up if it was clear, and I trusted his judgement and went through. I was a little cagey at first not knowing him, but as we had now ridden some considerable distance together, I trusted him and his judgement because of his grace and ability on a motorbike. After all the distance from the border to Dubrovnik was about 50 kms!

Unfortunately, I didn't get the chance to say hello, shake hands or even give a nod of appreciation to him or his pillion, as they turned off the junction before the one we wanted. It would have been a very nice end to the ride to have just had some contact and put a face to this exceptional rider. We took the next exit once we were all back together and it took us down towards the large port, where we thought we would be able to find a half decent hotel to stay in.

The jewel in the crown - Dubrovnik

There were some pretty big cruise ships docked in the port and lots of other boats too. There were people wandering around in the late afternoon sun and it was lovely to sit there and have an ice cold soft drink, while we looked for somewhere to stay on one of the phone apps. This place was heaving with people as we sat there chatting. We found a hotel about 100 meters away and went to enquire.

It was a lovely hotel but they didn't have three rooms, so that was out! We then started to look at some places at the other end of Dubrovnik. We found one that was a lot cheaper and a little way out of town. We booked online as it looked okay, it was cheap but we decided that somewhere for two days, that was clean and dry, with electricity for charging our electrical gear would do the job. It was only a couple of miles away, so we got our gear on and headed out onto the busy roads to find the new location.

When we arrived, it was an old 1970's holiday hotel, probably exclusive in its day but looked its age now. It was run down and in need of some attention, a revamp would give it a much needed facelift. We would only be there for two nights anyway, so that we could get washing done, have a good rest, wander about, enjoy being right next to the sea and be ready for the next leg, after we'd had some R&R.

It was only €30 a night, so we were not complaining, it was Dubrovnik! We'd had a long, hot day and this place had air conditioning, we each had our own room, a shower, toilet and bed. What more do you need? We parked up outside the hotel, tightly parked to make viewing them a little difficult. The bikes were all running well, no issues so far, apart from the slipping clutch scare in Austria. I gave all the bikes a quick once over to ensure they looked OK and were ready to go in a couple of days time after our well earned rest. We unloaded our stuff and headed to our rooms to get changed and ready for a dip in the sea just 100 meters away.

Some time out

At the beach there was a lovely little area to watch the world go by. The sea was very clear, the beer was very cold and we sat and chilled out for an hour or two in the sun, relaxing and chatting about the great day's riding we'd enjoyed yet again. The views were lovely and we enquired where we could eat in the evening, we were pointed to a place across the water where there seemed to be a hive of activity and a lot of restaurants.

We still needed to find a bike shop to replace the Scala radio that had been broken off by the bird strike on Day 2 in Germany. As only Mike and I could talk to each other via radio and boy can he talk, I thought at one stage my ears were bleeding! I was also suffering with a sore shoulder so I'd booked a massage for 7:00 pm at the hotel next door for the following day. That would be a welcome treat to get rid of the knots and soreness that I was experiencing whilst riding.

After a really nice chill out on the beach, it was time to head back to the hotel, get a quick shower and change ready for dinner. We walked down to the main strip that was full of bars and restaurants. We chose one that overlooked the sea and had an ice cold beer followed by a beautiful meal and a bottle of cold white wine to wash down the fish and watch the sun set. After a few drinks and a natter we were ready for bed pretty early as it had caught up with us, but Mike decided he'd rather stay up and go and have some more beers in the bars on the strip, so we left him to it and headed off to bed. This two night stop in Dubrovnik was to chill out, catch up on sleep and rest so that we were refreshed, ready for the next phase of the trip.

Once back at the hotel room, it wasn't long before I was in the land of nod and in a deep sleep and ready for some down time over the next 36 hours.

Day 7 - Croatia (Rest day)

Date: Monday 12 June 2017

Weather:

Glorious weather, it was hot and sunny all day.

The Days Events - Our Rest & Recuperation (R&R)

Mike hadn't been impressed when he'd been shown his room the previous day. The bed had been slept in and not changed and there was something else wrong too. They did move him, they said they'd upgrade him to another room and when he got there it was exactly the same as the one he'd just vacated! Ginge had been kept awake all night by a dripping tap, he reported it and they said it would be sorted out. It never was and I'm sure it's still dripping now.

We'd had a pretty decent night's sleep, our washing was being done by the hotel laundry and all electrical stuff was being charged and sorted out. The SD cards were given to Ginge and he was transferring all the data onto his laptop.

What to do in Dubrovnik for a day

The morning of our rest day started quite early. We had breakfast about 08:00 am, which was a lie in for us and then ventured by taxi in search of a bike shop to try and locate a Scala radio for Ginge. The previous evening we'd been told where to find a big bike shop but when we arrived there it was a scooter shop that was very small in size and closed. We hadn't let the taxi go and directed him to take us down into the town instead, where we had decided to spend the morning only, as we wanted some chill out time and Ginge wanted to get on with creating the videos to date, as he was behind in his time frame to get stuff done.

The cable car in Dubrovnik

We had a walk around the old town to start with, taking lots of pictures and seeing the usual touristy sights. Mike had been here before and knew his way around so we let him take the lead until he got us lost! We had a gentle stroll around the harbour before the drone went up for a video opportunity and then we stopped for a cold fresh orange juice and a coffee before heading to the cable car. This gave us a better vantage point on the city walls and just appreciate the higher view where so many pictures of Dubrovnik were taken from. What a beautiful looking city from up high on the side of the mountain. You could see why they fought so hard to keep their 'jewel in the crown' during the conflict, as it now boasts over 2 million visitors per year.

Almost a quiet drink

We headed back down for one final stroll around the inner city walls and went to find a bar that Mike knew about which was on the coast. It was a pleasant spot that overlooked the waterway boating channel into the harbour and port. We found it eventually, cut into the rock, you would have just walked past the opening without a second thought if you weren't looking for it.

This was where Ginge had a disaster with the drone. He didn't calibrate it when we got there and flew 'Wander' (his nickname for the drone) up over the sea. It took a wobbly and started to fly out of control and headed out to sea and back again, veering around peoples heads but luckily not hitting anybody. It was obvious that it was trying to get 'home' which is the place it started from, but was not stable at all. It crashed into the rocks and was almost lost in the sea until Ginge scrambled down to the water's edge to retrieve it, oh dear that could have been such a different outcome. It was quickly packed away and didn't see daylight for the rest of the day.

We then went and grabbed something to eat on the move, rather than stopping in a cafe or restaurant where prices would be sky high. So a slice of pizza on the move it was and then we went to find a taxi to head back to where we were staying on the opposite side of Dubrovnik. It was nice and quiet where we were in comparison, so was a good choice for the relaxing time that we wanted.

An afternoon at the beach

When we arrived back at the hotel Ginge wanted to get on with the videos, as he was getting stressed about them and was so far behind, so Mike and I went to the sea front for the afternoon. They had a nice bar down there with sun beds and umbrellas. There wasn't any sand so it was pretty stony and rocky but the water temperature was lovely and it was a great place to go and chill out for a few hours and take on some lost fluids with a small beer or two.

I spoke to a very nice young waiter who said Croatia was still full of corruption. We discussed his job, his plans and talked about old times and me as a military man when I was based there for 6 months during the conflict. He said the north of Croatia and Slovenia were very poor and that most of the people headed south to work because that's where the tourists were. He was well educated and had a degree in engineering but was working as a waiter to make ends meet, until he could get a better job.

Mike was on the phone sorting out some personal stuff along with doing a route plan for the following day, so I grabbed a sun bed and took time to relax and reflect on life. I was also writing a short blog everyday about each day's events and took a couple of hours writing that and logging some of the things that had happened over the previous couple of days. My massage was booked for 7:00 pm, so at around 6:30 pm I went to get changed and ready for that, as it was a bit of a walk and I didn't want to be late.

A treat in Dubrovnik

I was introduced to a very petite young lady who was going to look after me, she didn't speak much English but I got it across that my shoulder was sore and I wanted it sorting out. She said she understood and got to work, it was a bit gentle for a sports massage and I felt it could have been deeper but then again I was in pain so perhaps that's why she didn't go too hard. It felt better for the rest of the night and I thought it had done the trick.

We met up at 8:30 pm to head down to the same place as last night for dinner, Ginge was a tad stressed out as things in the video editing hadn't gone to plan. He was getting himself vexed by how far behind he was and we could see it was interrupting his time on the trip. We didn't make the decision for him but said it wasn't right that it was taking over his spare time and was becoming a big focus of each day, this trip was supposed to be enjoyed not endured!

We found somewhere to eat on the strip of restaurants and bars. The food was okay but not up to the same standard as the previous evening. The company was good though and we had a laugh and joke as we enjoyed the rest of the evening. Mike didn't want to finish as early as Ginge and I, so he headed off to a local bar for a few more beers and to watch the football that was on the big screen. Near the hotel Ginge and I stopped off for a nightcap before we hit the sack for a good night's sleep in preparation for the next phase of the journey.

I got back to my room and finished off packing so that I would be ready to have breakfast, load the bike in the morning and check out and be ready for the off. I felt pretty good now after a bit of time to relax and was looking forward to a good night's sleep. It couldn't have been long after my head hit the pillow that I was out like a light and counting sheep.

My summary of Dubrovnik

We'd had a good time in Dubrovnik. Plenty of laughs, drank a few beers in the old town, saw some great sights and felt a bit of the history as we'd wandered around. Watched young people enjoying themselves, flinging themselves off rocks in the heart of the city, been up a cable car and viewed the city from above and really had a relaxing time. The time I'd spent there had been too short and really not long enough to get a good feel for the city, so I would return in the future to spend more time to explore further. A nice city break, with a few guided tours to find out what really happened during the conflict would be worth every penny.

CHAPTER 9

Croatia to Albania

Day 8 - Dubrovnik to Theth
(Croatia to Albania)

Date: Tuesday 13 June 2017
Depart time: 09:00   **Arrive time:** 18:30

Days Mileage: 170 miles
Fuel cost: £11.42 approximately

Route:
Dubrovnik (Croatia) - Cavtat - Topla (Montenegro) - Kotor - Tivat - Budva - Podgorica - Tuzi - Koplik (Albania) - Theth

Roads:
To start with in Croatia, the roads were congested and slow going but when we arrived in Montenegro it was fantastic scenery and the roads were quiet. When we headed inland the roads were very excellent. The Austrian guys we'd bumped into on a previous border crossing were right, they were brilliant roads the further inland you travel.

Albania had stunning views as we climbed up into the mountains towards Theth. The roads were okay on the main drags and turned into good single track tarmac in the mountains, before turning to gravel tracks and boulders.

Border crossing & Insurance:
Croatia to Montenegro was a slow process, no green card meant a charge of €10 for insurance before we could get in.

Montenegro to Albania was a shambles, it was congested and extremely run down. It cost €12.80 for insurance before we were let into the country.

Weather:
Very hot and sunny, up to 37 degrees.

Countries travelled & Currency:

▬	Croatia	Kuna	kn
▬	Montenegro	Euro	€
▬	Albania	Albanian lek	L

The Days Events - Ready to get going

After a well deserved day off it was time to get cracking with the journey. Fed, watered and well rested we were all up early and at breakfast just after 07:00 am, when it first opened.

Continental style breakfast, with the strongest coffee I've ever experienced (even comparing it to Greek and Cypriot coffee) and now wide awake, we finished packing our kit and loaded the bikes before checking out. It was a pity we didn't check out together because we were all charged different amounts. When challenged, the guy at reception was extremely obnoxious and refused to change the price - even though the 3 rooms were exactly the same. I gave him some earache and told him his hotel was awful and his service was shit. He really didn't care, the place had been built in the 60's and was extremely tired and run down. At least we'd had wifi, a dry place to rest, with a bed and electrical sockets to charge our electrical stuff, ready for the days ahead.

Anyway, we didn't let that spoil our trip. I'd told him it was shite but I'm sure that fell on deaf ears, as did the complaints Mike and Ginge had made the days prior. What could you expect? It was a cheap base for a well needed rest before continuing our journey.

It wasn't long before we departed and were headed south along the coast road. It wasn't that good in comparison to the earlier routes in Croatia but we were heading for another country, this time Montenegro. The road was quite slow and congested, probably because it was tourist country, there was an airport and lots of people in the area. It wasn't that far to the border and we arrived about half an hour after setting off. We took advantage of filling up before we got to the border as you never knew what the fuel situation was like in a new country, especially as you headed further south.

Crossing the border from Croatia to Montenegro

The border crossing was a bit of a chore, long waits in queues and the border guard had a proper look at the documents, passports, V5 and insurance. Ginge didn't get our arrival at the checkpoint off to a good start, as he upset the border guard by riding past. Oh dear, the guy put the barrier down, stopped seeing to Mike and marched straight out of his box over to Ginge. Oh no, he didn't look very happy at all! He told Ginge he had crossed the 'red line' without permission and should be arrested!

We soon had the matter under control by apologising and using our charm, humour and joviality (piss taking) to win him over. That was a close one, Ginge wasn't allowed to lead at the border crossings anymore. We had a laugh and joke with him and he said he trusted us to go and buy insurance before we passed through Montenegro.

Passports back in our hands, we headed to the building just up ahead on the right hand side, there were people there being fleeced as well. We had to show passports and V5's to the guy who was doing the insurance and in return we were given an official looking piece of paper as our proof of insurance to travel through Montenegro. There was a small charge to pay of €10 for fifteen days insurance, as the UK doesn't issue green cards anymore. This was just the first of many hassles we were going to come across over the lack of green cards and insurance. The air would become blue with our expletives regarding UK insurance companies throughout the rest of the trip.

We weren't given a receipt in the little makeshift office marked as 'insurance'. We had been told it would be €35 before we started the trip when researching the cost, so a mere €10 without a receipt was worth the entry in to the country. Besides we were just transiting and would be out of Montenegro by mid afternoon all being well. Ginge, on the other hand didn't have any issues at all, as he had German insurance, with a green card. Even if he wasn't covered by his insurance in the country we were travelling through, it was enough for him to show a green piece of paper and he sailed through every single crossing between countries without any problems at all.

A brand new country for Ginge, so the flag came out and we did the all important pictures and bits of video for our archives. It was also becoming a bit of fun as I ticked off my country list and shared our progress on social media. We took it in turns holding the flag and having pictures taken with the three of us together by any onlookers, if there were any about.

Riding a motorbike in Montenegro

The views in Montenegro were stunning, they were truly magnificent as we headed down the coast. We were blown away with the spectacular views as we travelled further south and rode around what looked like a huge lake, but it was salt water from a tiny inlet. Most of the journey around the lagoon was almost at sea level. It was beautiful, surrounded by mountains with great views in all directions. Where to look first so as not to miss anything. We stopped for photos but the pictures didn't do it justice somehow, we actually thought these views were good, but wait until we headed inland and into Albania. There was a ferry that cut out a big chunk of the road but we were there for great roads and views, not for cutting short the chance to ride in this beautiful place.

We went past Tivat (an upmarket place on the inlet), the views when we looked back across the water from where we'd just been, were as good as when we were over there, riding towards where we were, breathtaking - these Countries just keep giving and giving in every way.

Leaving the lagoon we headed towards Budva. The views were pretty good and we rode past two holiday resorts that we'd never heard of before, property from only €9,000 upwards. As we turned left inland we saw the huge mountain we were about to climb and drop over the other side towards Podgorica.

As we got to the top of the climb and looked back over the two coastal bays below of Budva and Bečići, double wow, absolutely stunning. We admired the views yet again before continuing with the journey. The roads were well tarmacked and pretty fast but we were going uphill and didn't push too hard as we were still trying to observe the views far below and were aware of the big drops just a few metres to the right.

The riding was slow in places because of the terrain and holiday traffic, but it all added to our experience. We wanted to see some of the land we were negotiating and not just grey tarmacked roads. When the roads did improve they were brilliant, they matched the views but when the roads were poor the views more than made up for it. The roads at times were fast and sweeping to tight corners for miles and miles, once we were inland. The last leg on approach to the next border took us past a huge lake on the right hand side, it was sunny and had beautiful views for the last stretch.

We took advantage and fuelled up while we were still in the land of the euro before arriving at the Albanian border.

Crossing the border from Montenegro to Albania

The border crossing was a bit of a chore, long waiting times as people were checked thoroughly before being allowed to enter the country. If you thought the border at Montenegro was poor, you should experience the one going into Albania!

Unorganised chaos is the best description, it seemed to be every man for himself. People pushing past, impatient, border guards shouting and gesturing to people. It was dirty and not a nice place to be waiting for over an hour in the soaring heat. It was an eye opener, a really run down border crossing that looked like it was being done up but also appeared to have been in this state of disrepair for years.

We'd seen 37 degrees on the bike thermometer and were jaded from the heat. We edged forward a car length every 5 minutes or so. It was hot and uncomfortable but we made the most of it chatting and discussing 'nonsense'.

Eventually we got towards the front of the queue, having spoken to a few locals who were interested in our journey and wished us well before we were called forward. Hot and sweaty, we were at the front of the queue. We kept Ginge safely behind us as Mike and I handed over our passports, "Where is your green card?" we were asked. "We don't get them in England anymore!" was our reply, "You can't come through without insurance" we were informed. This time the insurance guy was ready to pounce, walking up and down the queue of traffic looking for easy targets.

We were told we needed to go to the little office to pay for insurance, so went off to pay our €12.80 premium. We were not even offered any change from the €13 he took from us. I wondered how many vehicles he saw a day and how much extra he earnt with his little scam each year. He probably took more this way than he earnt, a nice little bonus from this corrupt process.

We were expecting this to be honest, as we'd researched in the early stages leading up to the trip and had already been told about buying insurance at the borders. The prices were clearly shown so there was no way of being charged different rates, although I expected it was inflated prices anyway, just to grab a few extra quid out of travellers.

Riding a motorbike in Albania

We were well into the next day's ride now (according to the initial itinerary) as we'd made really good time. We decided to carry on to Koplik and then head up the mountain. It was only half an hour or so to ride down to the foot of the mountain, the roads were pretty boring and when we arrived in the town it was pretty grim, run down and not very clean and was a bit like every man for himself. Road rules were something that were loosely followed.

After such a difficult day with hot weather and Mike not doing so well, we decided to stop for a quick lunch break and to get some fluids on board. We stopped at a place that had lots of Russian looking memorabilia all around the bar and restaurant. It was a very odd place. The food wasn't great but we managed to get water and something to eat. It was strange to see and very nostalgic for the people here I'm sure, but it wasn't for me.

Continuing, we reached the turning that would take us left towards the beautiful mountain range, now all of a sudden the roads and tranquility took us to a different place physically and mentally. It was quiet, peaceful arable land with very few people around. Starting off on a single track road we continued on the most amazing route. The views were to die for heading cross country with the mountains before us, if we thought we'd had it good before, we were in for a real treat now!

Ladies were on their hands and knees working in the fields, acres and acres of lavender, the smell was amazing and fresh. The flat plain was once again surrounded by mountains and our route was taking us straight towards the big one in the distance. It was slowly growing bigger by the second, although it was still a long way off.

We passed a newly built jail in the middle of nowhere, certainly no place to run to from here. It seemed an odd place at the time but it was well out of the way.

We came across shepherds herding goats on the road and in the scrub land either side, there was a really old woman with a flock of sheep around her feet - like they were her children, donkeys walking along the road on their own, cows being moved from one place to another and to top it all pigs wandering around the road too. We'd certainly had a treat so far and witnessed something special.

When we stopped Mike said he'd been stung by a bee, and when I looked he still had the sting in his lip, so I pulled it out for him and slapped on a load of aloe vera. We thought this would do the trick as Ginge had been stung on the ear a few days previously and we'd done exactly the same to him and he'd not mentioned it since.

Alluring Albania

The valley floor was getting narrower, old houses were dotted around on the hillside and a group of caves overlooked us from high on the hills. I'm sure they would have been used as shelter or even living space in years gone by. They were probably used now by the animals roaming the hillside in the depths of winter to stop them freezing to death when the snow came down.

Although this was a beautiful place now, I thought how hard it must be in the depths of winter's grip, when the snow was falling and temperatures were well below freezing. The road had very good tarmac, it almost looked new, with snow capped mountains as a backdrop. It was green everywhere on the low sections of the mountains, with what looked like huge slabs of marble dotted about high up the slopes. Locals looked pleased to see us when we passed, waving and stopping to say hello if we stopped for any reason.

This place was getting better by the minute. Up to the top of the mountain was a good tarmacked road, it was narrow and not very fast but the views were spectacular. We didn't want speed anyway as it was treacherous and one false move and we'd be down a very steep cliff on the right hand side! Slow and steady was good and we were happy to enjoy the views and not the speed, we took the opportunity to stop and take pictures and talk about how good it was.

Wow, just wow! When we reached the top and looked back down on the pass, we had it all to ourselves, not many people travelled here. We arrived at the top and the tarmac changed to gravel as we crested the summit and then saw what lay behind and ahead of us. It was just perfect and beautiful, we were blown away.

On top of the world

As the tarmac changed to gravel, we had two places to choose from that we could head to ready for tonight's stop over. We decided on the closest option as it had taken a couple of hours to get here and was getting late. We didn't want to put tents up in the dark so rode a couple of miles to the first campsite area that had a bar/food cabin. When we got there we camped on a flat level grassed open area that had been levelled and maintained. A wooden hut was just on top of the hill overlooking the most magnificent view and there were a few small log huts that looked like mini houses.

We later found out that this was where the people who worked here slept. There were more being built and these were going to be accommodation for tourists eventually, along with proper shower and toilet facilities that were being built too. The other alternative was to move on and wild camp elsewhere, which we all decided against.

We chose to stay where we were at 'q. e T'thores' (name of place in the mountains) as they had cold running water, toilets and beer. At last, home for the night, we'd purchased food earlier on, so we were not going to go hungry anyway. We soon realised there was no phone signal and no wifi - we were off the radar for the next 12-14 hours, but people back home knew we were okay as we'd been keeping in touch with them earlier on, before we'd got to the top of the mountains. It would be a better night without the distractions of Facebook and messaging people.

The tents didn't take long to set up, we got sorted quickly and camp was made for the night. As we were settling down a few of the locals came over with an Albanian flag, so that we could take some pictures, one of them spoke very good English. We found out that he was a local English teacher but had never visited the UK. The owner of this place was from England and lived in London. How the hell do you get to own a mountain, we thought. It was being built up, shower block and washrooms, more cabins for sleeping in and obviously was going to be on the tourist trail for the future.

A very warm welcome in Albania

They invited us for dinner, as they had already prepared the table and surrounding area for eating. We knew this as Ginge had been asked not to walk all over the mats with his boots on, as it is customary to take your shoes off. There was a low level table with cloth and rugs on the ground. You sat on the floor at a table no higher than 12 inches, cross legged and ate with your hands, this was the local, traditional way of eating. Although knives and forks were supplied, I left mine where they were and ate like the locals. It seemed that our hosts got more pleasure from ensuring we had a great time, than they would if they had joined us.

Our food was local kid (baby goat), that had been prepared the previous evening and cooked on a spit, fresh goats cheese and yogurt, a salad, local potatoes with cow's cheese melted on top and a piece of pork that had been prepared almost a year ago by salting and air-drying. A couple of beers washed it down as we thoroughly enjoyed true Albanian style cuisine, a completely new and fantastic experience. The total cost for the whole night was a meagre €40 for camping, food and beer for all three of us, we thought it should have been that each!

What a magical end to a fantastic days riding with magnificent views and lots of firsts for all of us. Mike cracked open the bottle of wine that he'd bought when we were leaving Croatia. I told the story of the drunken nights I'd spent in my Army days when I was based in Ploče. We'd use empty water bottles and get them filled up with local red wine from the side of the road at small shacks, and buy huge watermelons too. The wine seemed so much better in those days, although it was probably pretty awful, but nonetheless Mike had decided to buy a bottle to sample it at some point in the future and tonight was the night!

Chilling out on top of the world

We made a fire, drank the red wine, that wasn't as good as the memory had been and chatted to each other and to a couple who were travelling through in a Land Rover. He was from Italy and his girlfriend was from London. We talked for a good hour and she told us that she wanted to do her bike test and how they'd met each other on a flight some years ago and their relationship had started.

He told us not to do the off road section that we were planning for the following day, as it was too dangerous. Because Mike was a little unsure anyway, we decided to seriously think about it and make a decision in the morning, depending on the weather and feelings that we had about the task ahead.

As it grew darker we watched the night sky and the stars became brighter, spotting satellites whizzing past at high speed, shooting stars and all in a quiet and peaceful mountain setting, with no noise or light pollution.

We had fallen in love yet again, this time with this part of Albania. It was getting cold so I asked our hosts for a blanket as I didn't want another uncomfortable night with very little sleep. They gave me a blanket that was so thick, I'd never seen one like it before. Folding it in half it covered the bottom of my tent and I could wrap the other half over the top of my sleeping bag and still have some left over to create another layer. I was sure this would keep me toasty in the depths of winter but for tonight I was going to be nice and cosy. Needless to say it was far too warm that night and the blanket had to come off to let me cool down. A great night's sleep was going to be had by all, to round off an absolutely brilliant day.

CHAPTER 10

Albania to Macedonia

Day 9 - Theth to Struga
(Albania to Macedonia)

Date: Wednesday 14 June 2017
Depart time: 08:00   **Arrive time:** 16:00

Days Mileage: 260 miles
Fuel cost: £19.18 approximately

Route:
Theth (Albania) - Koplik - Shkodër - Lezhë - Tirana - Elbasan - Struga (Macedonia)

Roads:
The route down the mountain was the same as the route up because we decided not to do the off road section on the grounds of safety. The main roads in Albania were not great but as we rode east the roads got much better, they meandered their way alongside the Shkumbin River before reaching Macedonia.

Border crossing and Insurance:
The border was a very quick process as there was very little traffic, show passport and vehicle documents but without a green card the insurance cost €50 and lasted for 3 months. We knew before we set off that we were not covered in Macedonia and there would be an insurance charge at the border.

Weather:
Chilly at first in the mountains but soon warmed up and stayed hot and sunny all day.

Countries travelled & Currency:

Albania   Albanian lek   L
Macedonia Denar   ден

The Days Events - A rough start

T he day started early with Mike looking a little jaded and swollen, he'd been stung the previous day and I'd pulled a bee or horsefly sting out of his lip. By 06:00 am it had swollen tremendously and was looking pretty bad. He was in need of some medical treatment or antihistamines to reduce the swelling. He hadn't had a good night's sleep and was looking pretty rough from the ordeal.

We got ourselves ready with a wash and shave in cold running water and started packing our kit. Mike wasn't whining much at all and said he was okay to ride, our first stop was going to be a nearby chemist to get some medication for him.

We were soon packed up, had a quick cuppa and I reluctantly handed back the blanket that was made for cold weather in the mountains, as it had given me the most wonderful night's sleep. We said our goodbyes and once again we were on our way but it wasn't long before we were stripping off some clothes from the chilly start, as it was hot already in the sun and we were descending this magnificent mountain.

We had decided not to risk ourselves or the bikes, as one of the comments was "if you get it wrong you will fall to your death!" We weren't too worried about ourselves, but how could we continue our trip without our motorbikes! Being as Mike was in a shit state, we would have changed our plans for the off road section anyway, as he just wasn't up to riding that kind of terrain in his present state. Even if Mike had been fit and well, we would have been airing on the side of caution as he really wasn't a confident or skilled rider and would have struggled. We could do without accidents, broken bones or bikes in the middle of a mountain range. We weren't even sure if this country had air ambulance or helicopters to come to one's aid.

I usually hate backtracking and going back down the same road you've just ridden up but on this occasion I actually enjoyed the feeling of terra firma and some photography of the others riding the twisties down the Rruga Gjecaj Pass before I made my way down on my own. I got some video footage of Mike and Ginge heading down the mountain and also managed to get some good pictures too. Once they were out of sight I set off to catch them up.

After a great gentle ride down the same stretch of road and passing some cattle and other animals enroute, we were soon back together again backtracking down the lower section of the mountain. The views were still as stunning on the way down, I managed to get some more video footage of them both ahead of me as we rode through vast areas of crops and arable land.

Inland Albania was disappointing

It wasn't too long before we were on the main roads again, this time heading south. We got to some urban places and soon came to the realisation that Albania was starting to lose its appeal. What a stark contrast, beautiful places in the hills and mountains, with kind and gentle people, to raving lunatics in cars who bully their way around the normal roads. The road conditions weren't great and there seemed to be a fuel station every few hundred yards or so.

Roundabouts seemed to be an inconvenience for drivers and we still didn't know who had priority. We saw a guy going the wrong way on a really busy roundabout in a 4 wheeled disabled mobility scooter, in the middle of the lane. Mopeds and cyclists going the wrong way, heading towards traffic everywhere we went. They didn't wear helmets on their motorbikes either. It seemed a pretty dangerous place to be on a motorbike. It was chaos, unclean and mental - where's the way out!

The open roads were generally in poor condition, the car drivers lived up to their earlier perception and pulled out to overtake when you were riding towards them or pulled out to overtake while you were overtaking them. Not what we expected after our early introduction yesterday afternoon, where our praise was certainly justified. This was a very poor country and there didn't seem to be much in the way of a law of the land. We found a pharmacy in the first town we came to and Mike got straight into his new medicine to try and ease the swelling and pain. He was getting worse as the day progressed and we needed to get to our destination as soon as possible.

Ginge has an off before lunch

We'd been going for a while and needed to find somewhere for lunch, we tried staying on the main drags and when we arrived in Tirana, we hit the main road but the motorway was closed. We followed the detour and came across a roundabout where we had to turn left. Ginge was leading and as he banked over to the left he lost the front end on the shiny tarmac, I saw this and turned off the power and I started to lose grip too. Ginge by this time was sliding across the road at about 10 mph and I just managed to save the bike by steering straight towards the kerb. Mike managed to stop behind me and we helped get Ginge and his bike back upright and to the side of the road. The traffic was pretty good, they slowed right down and swerved around us. At least it allowed us to get ourselves sorted out without being hit by the idiots but nobody stopped to help us.

All fine, we were on our way again and stopped for a lunch break quite early as Mike was suffering a little more by this stage. We found a nice cool shopping centre in the capital next to the main road. This was a lucky find really as it had some good food and was comfortable for Mike. It wasn't in the centre but on the arterial route out of the city in the right direction towards where we were going, it was still a chaotic place to be riding. The parking attendants were really good though, they parked us up next to their hut and looked after the bikes while we went on our way to find some food. We left our gear on them, as we were happy that these two guys were going to look after the bikes, they took their job seriously and used their whistles to guide everyone in the parking area, us included.

We took an hour or so to give Mike a break and take on more medication and fluids as it was getting hot out there. The air conditioning was very welcome and they had lots of good food places in the shopping mall. Mike's face was actually getting worse and not better but he had doubled the dose and was trying to get the swelling down, as it was affecting the tightness of his helmet. After we'd all eaten we made our way back to the bikes to find everything in order and the guards gave us a nod of acceptance as we arrived back.

We got geared up pretty much straight away and on the road again. The road was pretty boring really but we were in transit to Macedonia and not too bothered about great roads as we'd done plenty of them. Mike just needed an early day and we were heading for a hotel and not camping to make it more comfortable for him, until the swelling went down.

Riding a motorbike in Albania

Once underway we turned left at Elbasan heading pretty much due east towards Macedonia, we were on a main road next to a river. The views were really nice and the road was good, we were on there for some time and passed many nice looking hotels and restaurants along the route. The riding was good, once we were away from the towns but the roads were not all great, but the scenery and views were as good as in the north of the country. It would have been nice to spend a bit longer exploring here though. It was a pity we were on a mission, as we would have been better stopping here for lunch to sample the local food and hospitality like we'd enjoyed the evening before, high in the hills up north. I'm quite sure it was only the towns and cities that were disappointing as we rode through some lovely looking places.

We headed away from the river and turned left towards the

border. There was a small place at the side of the road selling green cards. If we'd been thinking more clearly about what was going to happen in the future regarding green cards, we'd have stopped to at least enquire about the price of them. I'm certain this would have helped us with a more swifter border control, with little or limited hassle for the rest of the adventure.

On a whole though none of us were too keen on riding in Albania, there had been a number of road closures and lots of heavy traffic and road works. There was also a lot of police at the side of the road doing random stops, we presumed for the corrupt ones it boosted their wages and at one particular garage they added money to the fuel bill, of course when questioned it was met with the language barrier!

A chap on a motorbike riding next to us at one stage, told us to be careful of the idiots on the road as it was dangerous and then he sped off like a thousand devils were chasing him. We could see why they had so many accidents here and realised why they drove around in old bangers, they didn't seem to have any road rules at all. It is no wonder we can't get insured in some of these countries.

Crossing the border between Albania and Macedonia

We got to the border and it was a pretty quick process as there was very little traffic and found out we would be relieved of €50 for insurance, which lasted up to 3 months though. For some I thought that may be worth it, but for us, we were only going to be there for less than 24 hours. Unless we took longer to transit Macedonia and detour to Greece on an alternative route.

My question again, why have UK insurance companies stopped doing green cards? We pay enough for insurance, the least they could do was give added cover to loyal customers and add a green card to the insurance policy, so that the customer could print it off if they wanted to. Now with technology it wouldn't be difficult to add a PDF or add to part of the schedule an extra document that doubled up as a green piece of paper when printed off and said green card on it (whinge over).

Anyway, someone is €100 better off after Mike and I parted with some cash in exchange for a bit of paper, not sure what kind of cover we had though but it was enough to gain entry and as Mike needed to get some rest and possibly some medical attention were were happy to get on our way.

We were never really supposed to go into Macedonia, it was never part of the route. We were going to head straight down the coast into Greece and then along the coast to Turkey, but being as I had made it my mission to do '20 Countries in 20 Days', I'd suggested we detoured and cut off a chunk of riding too. We were all in agreement as we wanted an adventure and to experience as much as possible whilst on the trip. It turned out to be a better judgement call with Mike getting worse by the hour.

We stopped for the usual picture and video opportunity and after the photo shoot with the flag, as required by Ginge we set off again. The roads started to improve and we only had a very short journey to do to get to the first major town in Macedonia. It was just over 10 miles to Struga which was a town on the north side of Lake Ohrid.

Arriving at the destination

We headed straight there, found a hotel that was a little old looking but well presented, clean and tidy. I went and enquired about room availability as we hadn't booked anywhere or even looked on the internet. A very nice looking reception and a lovely lady, who looked after us extremely well, gave us an option of rooms and views but to be honest the place was nice enough and we were not in the mood to go wandering around other hotels for saving a few quid. I went back out and told the others and gave them the room options while I got my stuff off the bike.

Once we had checked in the receptionist told us that we could eat in the hotel that evening without charge as it was courtesy of the hotel. We were told to park our bikes next to the front door for security reasons. I doubted they had many issues with bike theft here but it was reassuring that they liked bikers and were interested in our adventures so far. We also had a quick lesson on learning a few words in their language, so that we could at least say please and thank you. Most of the staff we came across spoke very good English and were really happy to welcome us and help us have a good stay in their hotel.

We went straight to our rooms, got changed and went for a quick swim in the pool. There was a huge lake less than 100 meters from the pool but we were just happy to be there in one piece with Mike and start to relax and try to get his swollen face under control.

We had a beer and then headed to the room for a shower before meeting up for dinner in the hotel. We had a good buffet style dinner with a very nice bottle of wine and discussed what we were going to do the following day. We decided that if the swelling hadn't gone down Mike must go and see a doctor or head to a hospital, to get some kind of IV medication to help the swelling go down.

We had a pretty early night, finished with Mike heading off to bed and Ginge and I having a coffee to finish off the evening in a local cafe bar that was packed with locals and was really buzzing with nightlife. This was one thing we hadn't really got involved with, as we were happy to get to bed early and stay hydrated rather than go out pubbing and clubbing every night. It wasn't that we were not sociable but on a trip like this you needed your wits about you and concentration levels must be maintained. Alcohol and late nights caused more problems than they solved, especially in this heat and terrain.

We had decided that if Mike was still bad in the morning then he'd be off to hospital and we'd check in for another night to give him a chance to get better, as his helmet was getting tighter with the swelling and it was uncomfortable. The tablets he was pumping down his neck were not helping and he was in need of medical attention. A typical bloke trying to tough it out but it could end pretty badly if the poison went further into his system or he had an accident because of the pain or if the swelling affected his eyesight.

I got to the room and I still had a few daily logs to create, so I set about doing them before falling asleep. I just wondered what tomorrow was going to bring with the situation we were faced with!

CHAPTER 11

Macedonia to Greece

Day 10 - Struga to Stavros via Thessaloniki (Macedonia to Greece)

Date: 15 June 2017
Depart time: 10:30   **Arrive time:** 21:00

Days Mileage: 200 miles
Fuel cost: £13.36 approximately

Route:
Struga (Macedonia) - Ohrid - Bitola - Niki (Greece) - Florina - Edessa - Thessaloniki - Stavros

Roads:
Started off on some lovely twisty roads through Macedonia and into northern Greece, then got onto the main drag (A roads) and some fast motorway riding to get to a Greek ho**pital.**

Border crossing:
Going from Macedonia into Greece was easy and a simple process. The border guard spoke very good English, passports and V5 requested, a quick chat and were through.

Weather:
Cooler with a chance of rain to start the day, but as the day progressed it got very hot and sweaty.

Countries travelled & Currency:

	Macedonia	Denar	ден
	Greece	Euro	€

The Days Events - Change of plan

W hat a day today was going to be! We were allowed to change our minds on what we did and that was the benefit of not having any plans. There were absolutely no rules, we could do whatever suited us.

Seeing Mike first thing before breakfast wasn't a good start to the day. He became worse during the night and it was evident that his self medication simply wasn't working, or doing anything to help his situation. We decided straight away that instead of leaving Struga, we'd stay another day as Mike was in serious need of some help, not by us but medically. His condition was slowly becoming worse and his eyesight was limited with the swelling. A course of IV treatment was going to be the best thing for him, to get this bee or wasp sting under control.

After a discussion we checked in for another 24 hours whilst Mike headed to the local hospital. We offered to go with him but he was having none of it and said he'd rather go on his own. He didn't want any fuss, just to head off, get sorted and then come back was the plan, although I wasn't so sure it was going to be that simple! Ginge and I settled down to a nice relaxed day, planned what we were going to do and have 24 hours rest. Ginge went back to bed and I sorted out some routes for the next leg of the journey and thought that I'd have some fish soup for lunch. Apparently it was a traditional dish, served for breakfast up until lunch time, and then in the afternoon we were going to view some footage and look at the video camera stuff from a few days earlier in the Albanian mountains.

Just as I was getting comfortable looking at maps and plotting a route Mike called - it was all change. "I ain't going to this place it looks like Beirut!" he said, "The doctor doesn't speak English, so we are going to Greece."

All systems go, I headed up to wake Ginge, who was now in

bed asleep and we started to undo what had been planned. The booking was cancelled at reception, it was a good job we hadn't paid any extra money for another 24 hour stay. We started to get our stuff packed, the washing that we'd had done the night before was also returned but not very dry from the laundry service but we had it back nonetheless and by 10:30 am we were ready to go.

Thessaloniki private hospital

Mike returned and it seemed a bit odd what had just happened. He'd gone to the hospital and said that it looked bad and was full of old people dying on stretchers in the corridors and that the doctors didn't speak any English. We probed him about who he'd spoken to and what had been said and still didn't get a clear answer, except that he wanted to head to Greece. It appeared that he'd not actually seen a doctor but made his decision on the look of the place, but being as we weren't there it was Mike's choice not to be seen. So we made plans to get him to Greece and looked on the map, the largest place with the possibility of a private hospital was Thessaloniki.

We paid up for the previous night and left the hotel, the reception staff had been really good to us. We'd had good rooms, complimentary dinner the night before, good conversation over a coffee and one of them saw us off and wished us well for the journey ahead. Everyone we'd come into contact with had been interested in our exploits and how it was going, some had even started following us on social media.

Riding a bike in Macedonia

All packed up again and ready to go we set off using the sat nav as we wanted the most direct route to Greece as possible. Mike was not in a good way and we knew he needed medical attention to get the swelling under control. It was clearly getting worse and could end up being pretty serious. It wasn't too long before we were out of town and on the main road heading south-east toward Ohrid.

Riding around the lake was very pretty with mountains all around and with the threat of rain to come. There had been a few drops on our visors, so it was threatening to come down. It was a little cloudy and visibility was not great for the nice views that lay all around. The Macedonian roads were not the best and the driving was pretty shocking. The towns were an eye opener, where roundabouts were just something in the way, how they passed a test here I had no idea! We passed through smaller mountains, rather big hills in comparison to where we'd come from but the views were just as special (when we could actually see through the cloud base).

Like everywhere else we'd been riding, the roads seemed to be in a valley floor with at least a 1km plain at the base, surrounded by mountains, or perhaps it was just our chosen routes! The road was lined with various crops and fruit trees. It couldn't be that good to eat as it was so near to such a busy road with vehicle fumes added into the flavour!

We stopped to refuel and it would be our last stop before Greece. The guy spoke very good English and he explained that he'd learned the language by being a 'gamer' and playing with English speaking people in Europe and around the world. He said the common language online was English and everyone spoke it when playing games, we took his word for it as we didn't have a clue.

Crossing the Greek border on a motorbike

It wasn't long before we reached the Greek border, we'd had less than 50 miles to navigate and there wasn't too much traffic once we were out of the town. The border was a very simple process compared to other border crossings, passports, V5 and a quick chat and we were through. Getting that all important photo had become the norm and we knew the routine well, this was just an easy process without discussion. Flag out, video camera out, phones out, snap, snap, snap and we were soon on the move yet again.

Mike was bearing up ok, although I knew he wasn't right, as the Scala communication hadn't earnt its money today and he was very quiet. Normally he was a chatterbox and I had to remind him to concentrate on the road in the challenging spots. We did talk a little bit but nothing compared to when he was fit and well and not suffering with a swollen face looking like the elephant man!

Greece soon started to heat up, we'd enjoyed a very moderate temperature in Macedonia and now it was warming up big time. The further south we travelled, the hotter it got, it was approaching lunchtime too as we hadn't left until late. The roads were pretty fast and twisty at times. It was the same as many other places though, as we continued south - a flat plain spread either side of the road, lined by mountains and hills with lots of agriculture going on in the valley.

Crops, herbs, fruit trees, you name it and we'd probably ridden through it or past it. This was a part of Greece that holiday-makers didn't see. Their great food has to come from somewhere! The ride was pretty uneventful, we were on main roads to make good time after the late start as we needed to find the hospital and get Mike sorted out. We arrived in Thessaloniki and it was manic, bikes, cars, congestion, bad drivers, poor riding skills, two up and no helmets - this was a different world.

We asked various people along the way how to get to the private hospital. I didn't think it was easy to find but we were guided in the right kind of direction, I hoped. It was total chaos. Our aim was to keep asking people where to go and eventually we'd be close enough to locate it ourselves. At one point I was asking someone in a car and a young lady rider stopped close by and asked if we needed any help. I said yes please, so she pulled me over to the side of the road. Mike was chuntering (moaning) over the intercom while I went over to speak to her. She listened to me and found out what we needed and then said she would take us to the hospital. What a lovely thing to do I thought and said thank you every 5 seconds, she must have thought I was an idiot!

The chaos of Thessaloniki

She said to follow her and took us straight there without hesitation. It was the other side of town and she guided us through the traffic (sometimes I closed my eyes at the gaps she took) but she was a very good rider in all the congestion. We could barely keep up with her, she rode with confidence and ease. Her vision and spatial awareness was impeccable. So, I videoed her as she rode effortlessly through the traffic. It was a bit tricky, one handed, filming, changing gear and stopping but I managed it all the same.

We were just about to turn into the hospital grounds and there was a nasty accident, car verses motorbike. The road was closed, so Elena (the female rider) took us on an alternative route. When we arrived at the hospital, she spoke to the car park attendant, who kindly let us park up in a spot close to where his cabin was situated. He said the bikes would be safe there. She then took Mike into the hospital with Ginge while I stayed with the bikes.

She went in to help translate and make sure Mike was sorted. What a lovely young lady she was and what a wonderful thing to do. She shrugged it off by saying we needed help and it was the least she could do. She eventually came back out to the bikes and we chatted for at least half an hour. She was interested in our story and the route we were taking and gave us a few tips and routes to take us through Bulgaria, north of where we were in Thessaloniki.

Now we had a route back through Bulgaria thanks to her kindness and our chance meeting. I thanked her again and invited her to 'The Midlands' if she passed through when she was en-route to the TT on the Isle of Man. She accepted and we said fare-well, after another thank you and she was on her way to wher-ever she'd been heading before we interrupted her day. So, we'd made a new friend who rode, toured and looked good on a bike, perfect. We still follow each other's exploits on social media to the present day, she has also kindly allowed me to use of one of her professional photographs on the rear cover of this book.

Ginge came back out, having found a cafe. He was happy to head back inside as it was now really hot and he wanted to sit in the air conditioned hospital. We headed for a quick bite to eat and some fluid as we now knew that Mike was being sorted out with medication and could be some time. The bikes were safe where they were, but we still locked away valuables and money before we left them with the car park attendant. Being robbed right now would just be the icing on the cake - exactly what we didn't need!

The private hospital

As it turned out Mike was kept in for over an hour on two IV lines direct into his arms with different medication. One was a steroid to reduce the swelling and the other a strong drug to fight the infection. Unbeknown to us he was told to stay local and not to ride too far as he would feel drowsy and maybe not too well for the next 24 hours or so. He was told he would need to return if the medication wasn't working or if he had an ad-verse reaction to it.

When he came out we discussed our options and decided to ride 100 kms to our new destination at Stavros, for a well earned rest. Ginge and I had eaten and taken on fluids, Mike had taken advantage of being laid on a hospital bed and had a nap for just over an hour but was in need of some food and drink to get ready for the ride ahead of us. His swollen face had already started to reduce in size and he was feeling better already, imagine how he'd have felt if he'd have been seen to much sooner!

Blokes never cease to amaze me (I'm guilty too). He had needed medical treatment for over two days and decided not to have it looked at locally when it was a smallish problem. Now it had caused us a very real problem by crunching in the miles to get to an unknown destination in the hope of treatment. It might well have been better treatment in the area that he'd been stung, as they would have had an idea of what did it!

Time was getting on a bit now, it was early evening and we just wanted to get going on the quick 100 kms ride to our next destination. We hadn't booked a hotel as we didn't know what we'd be doing until Mike came out full of beans and said that he was well looked after and it had only cost him €75. We thought that was fantastic service and prompt action. I wondered how long it would have been if Elena (our Greek friend) hadn't been around to help us.

Riding to Stavros

The sat nav was set and we went on our way. With motorways and the fastest route programmed in, it wasn't long before we were half way there and passed two large lakes on the right hand side. It was a fast dual carriageway and looked like a motorway to me, but we didn't care as we were on a mission to get as fast as possible before Mike's medication really kicked in and caused us to have to stop. Mike was governing the pace and the distance, we were ready to stop whenever he gave us the nod.

We arrived in Stavros and rode straight down the main drag. We weren't too impressed to start with, as it looked a bit run down and quiet, but as we started to look around it began to have more appeal. A port right by the town centre and lots of hotels dotted about. We were approached by an old lady who asked if we were looking for somewhere to stay (in German). We said yes and within a few minutes Ginge, who was our German speaking dude, was looking at the rooms and giving the thumbs up for a cheap and cheerful stay.

The hotel we found was very old, run down and cheap. We were only there for the night and would be away early in the morning. For now Mike needed rest and we all needed a bit of food and a beer to celebrate the success of the medication. We grabbed a quick shower (very odd looking), it had an umbrella type curtain that pulled around it but was broken and so old it needed removing and chucking in the bin! The toilet floor flooded because of the shower issue. I got dressed and met the other two outside in a warm, muggy street.

We wandered up the main drag which looked busy. It was a nice place, dated but pleasant. We were just transiting and needed food and rest after the day we'd had. We found a nice little taverna and sat down to eat. We were given a really nice bottle of white wine along with a couple of bottles of water. The food was great, seafood for me and meat for Mike and Ginge, we had far too much food and waddled our way back down the road to our hotel. It was only a few minutes walk and we were soon back in our rooms and off to sleep. It had been a really long, hot and sweaty day in Greece, waiting around and a bit of frustration from the start because of the sudden change in our arrangements, but as we had no set plans we could really do as we pleased.

Hopefully Mike would be in better shape tomorrow morning after the medication, it seemed to be kicking in really well. He was almost back to normal by the time we headed out of the hotel for a late dinner and he even managed a beer or two, so he must have been feeling better. He was given some tablets that he needed to continue taking and only he was aware of what he had to do if things got any worse.

Let's see what the morning was going to bring.

CHAPTER 12

Macedonia to Greece

Day 11 - Stavros to Alexandroupoli (Greece)

Date: 16 June 2017
Depart time: 09:00   **Arrive time:** 16:00

Days Mileage: 180 miles
Fuel cost: £25.40 approximately

Route: Stavros - Kavala - Xanthine - Fanari - Alexandroupoli

Roads:
Great roads all day, followed the coast and then went off the beaten track. Found some smaller unrestricted side roads.

Border crossing:
N/A

Weather:
Warm with a chance of rain to start the day, soon warmed up as the sun burnt away the cloud.

Countries travelled & Currency:

     Greece   Euro   €

The Days Events - A relaxed start

We'd had a pretty late finish the previous night because of our arrival time. The food had been fantastic and we'd gone to bed late with full bellies. Stavros was certainly a nice little holiday place and the restaurants and bars had been quite busy as we'd wandered back to our hotel. We all slept pretty well and were up early after getting a good 6 hours or so sleep. My kit was packed and I was ready for an early breakfast at 08:00 am.

We made our way down stairs to the breakfast area and it was very quiet and quite eerie really, as we had the whole hotel to ourselves. There was nobody else staying in the hotel at all. Ginge had negotiated €30 for the night, including breakfast and we enjoyed the pick of where to sit to have our breakfast. We couldn't resist it to be honest, we chose a prime position on the front terrace overlooking the beach and sea on a lovely warm sunny morning.

Breakfast was served to us at our table and was a typical European affair, consisting of bread, toast, cheese, ham, a fried egg and coffee. Oh and slices of cake - very odd but Ginge enjoyed his couple of pieces as we sat in the sun discussing the previous day and the one ahead of us.

Mike was in very good spirits, his medication had worked really well. His face had gone right down and was almost back to normal, he was going to be on tablets for a few more days but whatever he'd been given last night had worked wonders. It wasn't going to be good for me if he was back to normal, as he'd be yacking away in my ear for the rest of the trip - I'd actually quite enjoyed a quiet few days!

After breakfast Mike and Ginge had another cup of coffee and I went for a stroll along the sandy beach. I left my flip flops on the sand and went for a paddle in the sea. It felt nice and warm and inviting and I enjoyed a few minutes on my own with my thoughts for 10 minutes or so before returning to catch up with the plan for the day. We all headed back to our rooms to finish packing before meeting up for our departure.

Saying goodbye to the two old ladies

The hotel was old, very old and was in desperate need of refurbishment and modernisation but it was clean and had wifi which was a must for modern day travellers. For the price though, it ticked all the boxes. With its location and size it could have been so much more and I'm sure that in 10 years time it will have been sold and renovated to a completely new standard and probably full for the whole holiday season.

Two old ladies owned it and were both still working on reception, not very hard but they were in their 90's and still going strong. I shouldn't think I'll be around in my 90's, so fair play to them for still being active in the hotel business. Time had stood still for these ladies and I'm sure they hated every minute of modern times. They only spoke a few words of English, so Ginge needed to be our spokesman as they spoke fluent German. We returned the front door key that they'd given us the previous evening because they locked the hotel early, perhaps that was why the hotel was empty!

We checked out and paid our dues. It wasn't a lot of money for the great nights sleep and hearty breakfast we'd had. As I started my bike up I remembered I needed fuel pretty quickly, it was showing just 8 miles left before empty and I didn't fancy risking it to the next town, so filling up was high on the agenda before anything else. We'd noticed a petrol station when we first arrived last night, so headed back out of town in the same direction until we arrived at the garage. It seemed the norm down this end of Europe for people to serve fuel to you, rather than you fill up yourself, perhaps it created more jobs. This was a big fill up and cost €29 exactly. I wondered how much further I'd have had to go until it stopped completely but wasn't going to risk it.

Today we only had 200 miles to ride, but with Mike on the mend it could be a long one if he needed to stop more regularly to have a rest and a break. Yesterday he'd been told to stay near the hospital in case he had any problems and also not do anything for a few days until the medication did its job. So we travelled 100 kms away from the hospital and were on the move once again. I believe it was a good job he didn't have a reaction or need medical help last night as he didn't tell us what the hospital had said until we reached Stavros, so you can imagine our reaction when we found out, the words 'fucking idiot' were amongst the few expletives we used to describe him and his lack of common sense.

Getting going

Petrol station done, we were all sorted with a full tank of fuel, I lead the first 80 miles of the day. We fell into line as usual, the riding was familiar. There were very few surprises now as we knew how each other rode, but now and again I'd have a 'WTF was that' moment watching the others riding antics. You couldn't take the instructor out of this biker that easily, I could switch off but when there were some dodgy riding techniques or crap overtakes they stood out like a big red flashing light! The route today was pretty straightforward, coast road to Kavala, then on to Xanthine towards Fanari and then finally to Alexandroupoli.

Our sat navs did not include motorways or toll roads, we'd removed them from our routes for a reason. They were very boring roads with very little scenery and you didn't really feel that you were seeing any of the country. You may as well ride on the M6 back home in England if you wanted to blast on motorways on nice sunny days. The best way to see any country is to get off the main roads and head for the smaller roads but because Mike had been suffering we had to use main roads for the last couple of days.

The first part of the day was quite boring really. It was on the coast but the roads were nothing like the coast roads in Croatia. We'd been spoilt, my inner thoughts told me as we rode! So I decided that it was time we headed inland for a better road. It wasn't long before we were off the beaten track after a few sat nav blunders and recalculating. It was much better and we got to see more of the country we were travelling through, especially after ignoring the sat nav long enough to allow it to recalculate time after time.

After riding inland through woodland on small, narrow roads with some really nice twisty sections for forty odd miles or so, we rode down towards Kavala port. Heading downhill into the town from an elevated road position looked very pretty as we approached the harbour. There were lots of small bike shops on the road into town, but it was probably because there were loads of mopeds here. They looked like small one man shops, with a thriving business by fixing and servicing mopeds and small bikes. It appeared that every other person had a moped as their mode of transport. As it's a hot climate, they are quick and easy to get around on, easy to park and probably really cheap for the locals to use.

Local cuisine and a break

We headed straight for the waterfront and stopped at a nice location for coffee and some water. I looked at the menu that was presented to us as we sat down and I couldn't resist trying the grilled octopus that was on offer. I wasn't really hungry but as we weren't there that long I took the opportunity to sample some grilled octopus as I may not get the chance again anywhere else in Greece. It was a good way to keep my trousers snuggly fitting (not tight) which of course stopped them from falling down. I wasn't fat, just cuddly!

After a good break, some tasty octopus, and a couple of coffees and some water, we took some happy snaps around the harbour. We had a chat about the next section that Ginge was leading, and got ready yet again. As we set off we saw a sign that said 'Constantinople 460 kms', so of course we stopped to take a photograph of it as it now felt that we are almost there, just one more run after a stop over in Alexandroupoli and we were at our final destination, Istanbul and Asia.

Ginge lead the way out of the town and onto the coast road a good way out of Kavala, his sat nav was also set up to not go on motorways or toll roads, but this time he had the shortest route. It took us on a really nice road after some time near the coast, it was a bit of a twisty start as we headed towards the Nestos National Park. There was a large lake on the left hand side of the road with deep blue looking sea to the right, this setting was just wonderful. So I took off to get ahead of the others and film them doing a ride-by while I videoed them on the move.

It was lovely to see sights like this, we were sure not many holiday makers stumbled upon some of the roads and views we were experiencing. That was the great thing about this trip for me, no fixed routes, no fixed days, no fixed timings, just ride when we ride and stop when we were tired. The only condition for the whole of this trip was that we needed to be back home by the end of June.

After we passed the lakes we went off piste (off the beaten track), the sat nav took care of the route, oh and what a plan it would turn out to be. This was truly unbelievable, more farming and lots of it, from olive groves to sunflower fields and everything in between. Even the roads were lined with beautiful flowers and hedges that were deep pink, light pink and white in colour, it looked beautiful (I was in touch with my feminine side), they were much nicer than our roads back home. There were all kinds of fruit trees, herbs and people working the land. It was a pity Ginge was on it (riding quickly) as I found it hard to record with my mobile phone in one hand and banking over around tight corners one handed, on narrow roads with very windy conditions. It was all part of the fun though...

The river crossing

Out of nowhere we came across a large ford, it wasn't deep but quite wide and a little slippery as we walked through to test it out! A truck was coming the other way when we first saw the crossing and because of its speed we thought it was about 2 feet deep, as the wash he'd generated was huge either side of his front wheels. We decided to check it out first as we didn't want to lose a bike in the drink, so we sent Ginge on foot whilst I filmed him. I was hoping he'd slip over and we'd earn £250 on 'You've Been Framed' but he made it back in one piece after setting up his video camera on the other side.

While Ginge was getting back on his bike, Mike was the first to ride through. I also set my video camera to film us riding through the ford so that we'd have footage from in front and behind. In hindsight it wasn't very clever as I also got my feet wet, as I had to walk back through the water to retrieve my camera. So Ginge and I both got wet feet but Mike came away from this little adventure unscathed and dry. Mission accomplished, all through the ford safely, with video footage of both front and rear shots, cameras back in their bags and off we went again.

More farming, more fields and more tiny villages where time had literally stood still for many years. Then another ford, this time small and very shallow. This one was child's play in comparison, in fact you could have mistaken it for a puddle, it was that small. There were lots of sunflower fields here, I'd never seen so many sunflowers in all my life, I wondered where the seeds would be heading?

Mike had the hotel logged into his sat nav. We had two options, we could continue on these small roads for another 25 miles or get to the hotel. We decided to get to the hotel, it hadn't been booked, so it was an 'on spec' visit and enquiry. It was a very nice Beach Hotel and Spa and luckily they had rooms for the evening and maybe for tomorrow night too, but that was just a maybe as they had a large hen party and also a wedding the following day. "Okay" we said, "we'll take them" as we needed and wanted somewhere decent to stay. It had a spa and that swung it for me, I was in need of a massage. We could always move on tomorrow if we needed to but for now this would be our luxury stop.

A well needed massage

I booked a massage as soon as we'd made the decision to stay, I needed one because I was still sore from the trip down. I got to my room and grabbed a very quick shower and went to find where I had to go. I had a really good massage but I needed more than one to sort me out. My shoulder and neck were still quite sore so booked in for the next day too. I didn't want to be sore for the rest of the trip, as this was only around the halfway point.

The rooms were good, the hotel was very pleasant and we needed a rest after the last few days of uncertainty with long days and challenging medical situations to deal with, that could have changed at anytime. After all we were supposed to have stopped 2 days ago to rest and get Mike back to normal but he just wanted to push on. It had worked out ok but could very easily have been so different.

After my massage I found out we were meeting up later on for dinner so I went for a wander around the hotel to see what was on offer. I found the pool, the bar and the beach. As I had my trunks on I went for a dip in the Mediterranean and had my very own little shingle beach all to myself and spent a bit of time just chilling out and watching a couple of young guys jump off the 10 metre cliffs. I dried off in the late afternoon sun whilst catching up on some social media stuff, before going back to the bar and ordering a cold beer.

I got another quick shower to get rid of the oil and salt water and met up with the others for dinner in the hotel, with a nice bottle of white wine that was recommended by the head waiter. It had been a long few days so we were ready for an early night. The other two left me to it whilst I sat outside writing a few entries into the day's log and it was only an hour or so later that I was ready to retire too.

It had been a great day, with some very interesting sights that not many visitors had the opportunity to witness. It had been an enjoyable trip so far and one I'd certainly recommend to any biker who wanted an adventure. You didn't need an 'adventure bike' to have an adventure, you just needed a bike, some good company and an open mind and you'd have loads of fun and a great trip.

The rooms were comfortable and the beds were like sinking into clouds, it wouldn't be long before I was zonked out and sleeping like a log.

Day 12 - Alexandroupoli
(Rest day)

Date: 17 June 2017

Weather:
A very warm morning but turned into heavy rain and thunderstorms in the afternoon and early evening, still muggy but a welcome drop in temperature.

The Days Events - A well needed rest

The day started as usual by waking up early and adding yesterday's events to social media. I wasn't in a rush to get anything done, as today was a full rest day and even if Mike had said he wanted to go somewhere else, Ginge and I would have overruled him and stayed where we were for another 24 hours anyway.

We met up and had a fairly late breakfast (for us) at around 08:30 am. After breakfast the other two went off to do their own thing and I sat by the pool for a few hours catching up on admin and writing, as I was now 4 days behind writing up the logs of the day's events. It was mainly due to late night arrivals and some full on riding that had taken all day, along with some last minute unscheduled changes.

It was fairly peaceful around the pool to start with and then a group of kids arrived for what seemed like someones birthday. There was a food area prepared and lots of females bringing their children to join in. I didn't hang around too long when they started jumping in the pool and soaking my dry maps with all their splashing. It was getting grey and overcast by now and I'd enjoyed a good hour of chilling on the sunbed anyway, so off I went indoors near the bar.

Mike was now pretty much sorted out but still needed some rest as the sting had given him more problems than first anticipated. It wouldn't do him any good trying to struggle on whilst being unwell, he just had to plod on through the process of getting better. In the long run it would affect him as it had already had an impact on the trip so far, with late arrivals and changes to the itinerary, to compensate for the horrendous sting that had caused his issues. A well needed rest was required by us all before the next 5 or 6 days riding and long slog back through the rain that was forecast for the next 2-3 days as we headed in and out of Turkey.

Mike had cracked his phone and was off on his bike to try and find a place that could repair it and put a new screen on for him. Ginge was in his room staying out of the sun and working on the next episode of the video that he was producing for the tour. We met up and had a late lunch in the hotel as we were not that hungry at midday. After we'd eaten I took my SD cards and phone footage to Ginge's room, so that he could transfer all the files over to the computer he'd brought with him.

During the afternoon we ensured all the electrical goods were fully charged and ready to go for the following day when we would arrive in Asia. The rain started after lunch and it was torrential, thunderstorms, lightning and really heavy rain that put paid to any outdoor activities. All the kids came back in doors and disappeared as there was nothing else to do inside, after they'd come away from the pool. This was in for the rest of the day so we just spent the time chilling out and catching up on rest.

Another well needed massage

Because my massage was short the day before, I'd booked a full hour so that I could get my shoulder and back sorted out before the rest of the trip. It was booked for around 7:00 pm, which was pretty late but we'd eaten late at lunchtime so a late evening meal would be in order after I'd been tortured with a sports massage. I turned up on time and had a really good massage. I was a bit taken back when she told me to take my pants off and lay face down on the bed, I didn't want that kind of massage I thought! She saw my reaction and turned around to save my blushes. It was the best massage I'd ever had. I had a full body massage and it did me the world of good and had me sore for the next few hours but after a good night's sleep I'd be ready for the next phase.

We met up afterwards for a beer and chat to discuss the next day. We weren't really that hungry for another big meal and it was a buffet style affair anyway, the same as we'd had the previous evening. So Ginge went off to bed and to get on with what he was doing, while Mike and I had another drink and a snack from the bar. It was to soak up the beer really rather than to fill a hungry belly.

It wasn't long before we were also ready for bed, so after we'd finished our beer and snack we headed off to our rooms. Ginge and Mike had upgraded as the hotel was full and they needed to change rooms, as we were staying in the hotel for another night. It wasn't much more money and they didn't mind moving to the other end of the hotel after the first night. I also thought it was a bit quieter over there with a sea view anyway. I stayed in the cheap room overlooking the pool. This was going to be our last sleep before we got to our destination of Asia and we'd soon be on the return leg.

I was looking forward to being back on the bike and on the road to be honest, as this seemed to be a wasted day, with the weather being so poor, as I'm not usually a sitting down, hanging around kind of person. But I could get used to this kind of stopover to recharge my batteries now and again! Maybe I'd bring this kind of break into my life when I got back home - 36 hours doing absolutely nothing except chilling out, eating, drinking and resting.

I headed back to my room, got sorted for bed and finished off packing ready for the morning. Ear plugs in, I doubted that I'd hear anything until the alarm clock in the morning anyway. A well needed rest day, but a day on the beach with lots of swimming in the sea would've been so much better.

CHAPTER 13

Greece to Turkey (Istanbul & Asia)

Day 13 - Alexandroupoli to Istanbul and Asia (Greece to Turkey)

Date: 18 June 2017
Depart time: 08:30   **Arrive time:** 19:30

Days Mileage: 180 miles
Fuel cost: £47.83 approximately

Route: Alexandroupoli - Keşan - Tekirdağ - Silivri - Istanbul - Bosphorus River - Üsküdar - ASIA - Istanbul (Europe side)

Roads:
Motorway pretty much all day, fastest way there as there were issues throughout the days ride.

Border crossing:

Greece to Turkey, not having a Green Card resulted in major problems at the border. We had to purchase insurance costing €220, as it was a Sunday but if we went back on a weekday it may have been as low as €60.

We had a 3 hour wait and major issues, as the insurance I purchased in the UK before departure stated Turkey as being covered. But they didn't accept written confirmation, only a green sheet of paper that is recognised as a green card!

Weather:
A cloudy warm start, after the border it got a bit cooler towards Istanbul and then into heavy rain. The rain eased off and the day finished a pleasant 20 degrees.

Countries travelled & Currency:

	Greece	Euro	€
	Turkey	Turkish lira	₺

The Days Events - Today's the day

T he day started like every other. We got up early, packed our bags and met up at a designated time for breakfast. It was never exact - give or take 5-10 minutes, and we enjoyed a good hearty breakfast before heading back to our rooms to finish off packing, which was now the same daily routine. Then it was just a case of finishing off loading the bikes and taking some happy snaps or a bit of filming and then checking out. Today the bill was more expensive for me, as it was a nice hotel and I'd enjoyed two very good massages, I was now ready to embark on the next phase of our trip, pain free.

We got the bikes loaded up and were ready for the off and the final leg of our outbound journey. It wasn't long before we stopped at the first garage to refuel, as it was showing 40 miles to empty on my fuel gauge. My bike was definitely the one that did the least miles and not wanting to risk it, filling up early was a certainty. This also allowed Ginge a quick stop off to purchase some champagne ready for the celebrations later today, when we arrived on the Asian side of Istanbul.

We also looked for and hoped to find a local bike shop that was open for Mike, he wanted to buy a cheap helmet for the rainy days ahead, as he wasn't keen on riding in darker situations with a black visor. I didn't blame him really, I wouldn't want to ride in poor light conditions when it was raining with that black visor. Anyway, as it was Sunday they weren't open, or we were too early and they were yet to open, but we suspected it was the former as they didn't all open at weekends, because in this part of the world family time was much more important to them.

As we rode through the town it was very quiet, it wasn't even 09:00 am yet. We headed straight for the motorway and were Turkey bound in no time at all. The motorway was only a couple of kms from the town centre. The road was extremely quiet for a motorway, and was poorly maintained, with lots of potholes and a poor riding surface for more than half of the 30 mile journey. It was apparent that visitors didn't think much of the journey to Turkey because the road was appalling. There were different sections that were old and in desperate need of attention but I supposed they weren't bothered as it seemed to be little travelled on and we didn't see many other vehicles on it in either direction.

Chaos at the border

When we arrived at the border, it was absolute chaos. There was a huge line of trucks, hundreds of them just sat there waiting in line. I was glad I wasn't a truck driver as I rode past, pretty sure they were just being messed about for no reason! As we filtered our way to the front, I wondered what was in store for us, if this was the way they treated trade going into their country.

Waiting in the queue was easy as we'd done it so many times before, it was just a case of what nonsense we came across and this was going to be no exception. Getting through the first few checkpoints from Greece into 'no man's land' was no problem, but as went through the different sections to get through into Turkey, the insurance guys turned up!

What happens as you leave a country is that you end up going through their process to leave and is a pretty easy transition to be honest, as they clock you out of their country and then you go into a 'no man's land' between borders and start the process of going into the next country. That's when it causes the most problems if you don't happen to have a Green Card!

"Green Card", was the only English the border guard said as I showed him my insurance documents, as I'd already paid for the UK company to cover me in Turkey for the whole month of June. I hadn't got specific dates as to when we'd be there because the trip was open to change due to our circumstances. The border guard continued with the 'Green Card' stance, a little bit like the English who shout loudly and slowly to make themselves understood to foreigners. This wasn't going to get us anywhere I thought, Mike knew he'd have to get insurance and was sent off to get it from the 'Duty Free shop', a strange place to be sent, but off he went in search of the Insurance place.

Green card issues

I had asked my insurance company for a Green Card several times prior to the tour and been told that they didn't issue them anymore. Even my broker had come up against a brick wall when he had requested one and was told the same thing. However, it was an internationally recognised insurance certificate that everyone in Europe referred and adhered to, except the British Insurance companies as they knew better! Anyway, I'd decided that I'd made my payment in the UK and was not going to buy any insurance for just 24 hours in Turkey.

Mike had been given the run around and sent back to the checkpoint, so again we asked the border guard where to get insurance and he said exactly the same thing, only this time we knew it wasn't true. So together we headed off in search of the elusive insurance person and wandered around the main building unchallenged and ended up at the opposite end of the building. There she was, in a huge room, stuck in the corner with just a chair, desk and a computer, and the smallest sign you've ever seen that said 'Insurance'. We walked across and asked if she spoke English and her reply was blunt, abrupt and angry, "NO" - was her answer.

We spent some time there trying to establish what we needed, Mike gave her his details and documents and then 10 minutes later she said he owed 900 Turkish Lira for 15 days cover. "WHAT," was Mike's answer, "that's over €200" he gasped! She just shrugged her shoulders and Mike obviously felt that in order to go through the border and not be left behind, he'd have to make the payment. I said I wasn't going to pay it as I already had insurance.

Mike was relieved of €220 as they worked out the exchange rate. He handed over the cash because they didn't take credit cards. I wondered how much, if any, would be put through the books and actually used towards an insurance premium. I didn't think I'd like to put their insurance to the test. So, a little bit lighter of cash and with a feeling of being ripped off we got back on the bikes and we were off, to the final checkpoint to enter Turkey.

Trying to blag the border guard

I was going to try and blag my way into Turkey by just riding through with Mike, who now had the Insurance certificate and Ginge who had a Green Card. I was already insured and didn't see what the problem was because it was in black and white, besides the border guard had let us through and we were now home and dry. In other places we'd had to leave the bikes where they were until we'd paid for insurance. Only then had we been allowed to proceed.

We got to the final checkpoint and the guy was pretty grumpy and stern. He asked for vehicle docs again and we passed them over. Ginge was waved through and the barrier was lowered down very quickly in front of Mike and I. The border gate was closed to us, go back 'Green Card' was the only English he spoke. I didn't see the problem with Mike as he had insurance and then the guard kept repeating "number 2", we quickly cottoned on that the first checkpoint box was number 2, so I told Ginge not to proceed any further as he might not see us again!

So we went back again and Ginge was through on his own, as the

Germans weren't stupid like our insurance companies and recognised the importance of such a document. They only wanted to see the vehicle registration and chassis number printed on a green piece of paper! Our insurance companies needed to buck their ideas up, they thought they knew everything but were causing travellers a lot of problems and extra cost. This little border entry was going to cost me €220 for less than a two day visit into Turkey because of incompetent insurance people in the UK, who really didn't have a clue or even care that they were causing their customers grief and problems at foreign borders. They would when I presented them with my €220 bill and insisted on being reimbursed when I got home!

We headed back to the guard post and found out that Mike should have returned there to get his insurance certificate stamped by the guard. A process then took place where it showed on their system that the guard had seen the insurance and it was logged to that person and their vehicle details. Then at the next checkpoint the guard verified that the paperwork was in order and allowed the driver and vehicle into the country. That's why Mike had to go back, he had not had the process finished properly. I had no chance of getting through as I had been told to get insurance but hadn't bothered. They could see Mike was on the system but without the stamp he couldn't go past the final border guard.

A helpful local

Three hours later, hot and sweaty and back at the first border post, a really nice chap from Istanbul was near to where we were parked. He had a puncture on his Honda Deauville and was in a world of trouble. He'd had a brand new tyre fitted on his bike but the garage had not changed the valve and it had perished. A brand new tyre for the journey was great, but the incompetence of the mechanic who'd done the job, meant he was now in a world of trouble and not in a good place. We've all been there I thought!

He came over and asked us what was wrong as he'd heard us moaning about the way that they operated. He listened to what we had to say and immediately went to speak to the border guard. He was not very polite in his manner and was shouting the odds at the guy, who just sat there shrugging his shoulders. This biker spoke very good English and could also read it. He had my insurance in his hand and was showing and explaining what it said to the guard but after their discussion said to me that these guys were just peasants and couldn't read, he said they just wanted to see a green piece of paper and would be happy!

He wasn't able to do much but could explain the stupidity of the system we were faced with. He even went to the Insurance place and spoke to the girl there. He wasn't much calmer with her to start with, but she explained to him that it was a Sunday and that was the only rate they would give today. If we returned tomorrow it could be as low as €60. His advice was for us to return to Greece, have another night in a better hotel and enjoy the seafood, then return tomorrow to get a cheaper price. It wouldn't be much cheaper as the hotel would be €50, food would be €50 and the fuel would be around €30-40, which all added up and being a day behind schedule would not really make it much cheaper.

I was adamant I wasn't going to pay €220 for the rest of the afternoon and tomorrow morning in Turkey. So I decided I would turn around and go back into Greece, I'd spend the day on my own in one of the coastal resorts and then head up to Bulgaria in the morning to meet up with the other two around lunchtime. I had already paid for insurance in the UK and didn't feel like being ripped off with the possibility of my insurance company not giving me a refund.

Ginge at this point had made his way back to us. God knows how he'd blagged his way back in, the wrong way up to the first checkpoint, but he was now hot and bothered too. He asked what was going on and I told him my plan. He wasn't having any of it and said he'd pay for me, I declined but he was determined that I got to Asia with him. He wanted to pay by credit card but we told him he couldn't, so him and Mike put some money in the pot and paid between them. Ginge said "you're not getting this far and stopping here - I want you at the finish line with me." I said I'd pay them both back when I had the cash.

Reluctantly I handed over the money for a piece of paper that we couldn't read and said farewell and good luck to the biker from Istanbul, who'd worked with UK companies for over 25 years in different types of business.

On our way

Just one final stamp from the first border checkpoint to put me on their system and then off we went, as far from the border as we could. It had been an ordeal really and an experience, hindered by not knowing the language and not being able to ask anyone for help. You really were at their mercy to be honest.

As we got going again the road was lined with fields, all green and full of crops and vegetation. We didn't know what to expect but it wasn't this, mile after mile of open space, fields full of different crops and lots of huge petrol stations, similar to what you'd find in America. Very big rest areas and quite luxurious looking from an outsider's perspective.

All was going really well until we approached Istanbul. We were ordered to pull over into a police checkpoint and roadblock by some uniformed police, amongst them were a few plain clothed guys with AK47's and pistols. Just in front of us was an Italian biker called Fabio Salini (fabio vespapx) on a Vespa, enroute to Australia on his own. What a nutter, but fair play I thought!

They took our passports and disappeared with them. Whilst we were kept waiting for 20 minutes or so we had a chat with the

Italian guy and asked him about his travels and got some pictures with him. He asked about our trip, to be honest ours had almost reached its pinnacle, whilst his was very much at the beginning. Passports returned, they sent us on our way. We'd had absolutely no idea why we'd been stopped or what they'd done with our passports when the'd taken them away. Even though we'd asked, we were not given any explanation.

In the distance it looked like it was going to rain. As we got closer to the clouds we were aware that we'd be caught up in it, so we pulled over under a bridge. It started raining hard, so we got out our waterproofs and put them on. There were lots of bikers passing who were drenched, most without helmets or any protective clothing, just wearing jeans and t-shirts. As we were about to head off Ginge shouted that he had seen a warning light come on his dash that referred to tyre pressures.

It had to happen here

Yes, it had to happen whilst we were there, didn't it! As we were riding along I got him to edge forward slowly and saw a nice big piece of metal in his rear tyre. This was just what we needed, in the rain, in Istanbul, a puncture in his rear tyre. Mike suggested getting the ADAC (which was the European breakdown service) to come and sort it out and then head straight to the hotel. I thought this was a really odd thing to want to do, as it was the day we'd decided to go to Asia. But I had a better plan to put into action. "Let's repair it ourselves and get into Asia today," I said. That's what we'd come to do - get into Asia, besides we'd be hours waiting to get the tyre sorted out anyway. We could repair it ourselves temporarily and finish off the day as planned, after all we didn't have anything better to do!

We cracked on a while and the tyre was slowly going down, so we found a place that was safe enough to stop so that we could get on with the repair ourselves. Ginge got out the air compressor that he'd bought for the trip, whilst I removed the valve and squirted in the green slime I'd brought with me to plug any holes, then Ginge connected the compressor. But it didn't work, it fired into life for a nano second before stopping. We couldn't get it to work, oh shit, where's the garage? It would have been better doing it at a garage instead of trusting a brand new portable compressor. We were now in the position where we had a totally flat tyre and nowhere was open where we could get the tyre sorted out.

Luckily there were a few shops about, they were not open but had people milling about and upon asking around a guy said he had a compressor in his car. He came over in a small van with the compressor, a young lad who was about 12 insisted on doing it but he wasn't getting any air into the tyre. So I assisted and made sure it was working before they got too pissed off and wanted to leave, as the driver seemed to want to be on his way.

We blew up the now flat tyre and hoped that the gloop was going to work. After spinning the wheel it was obvious it wasn't working, so we used the centrifugal force of the tyre spinning in first gear to get the green gloop to where it needed to be. Good, that had done the trick and we thanked our helpers before they departed. They'd caused a traffic hold up trying to help and was probably the reason they'd seemed so impatient to leave.

I'd already used one half of the gloop in the tyre of the chap at the Turkey border, so it was a good job I'd kept the rest, as it was now a life saver for us and we were on our way again. A few minutes into the ride with constant checks, we established that it had done the trick and we were once again Asia bound. It wasn't the problems that you encountered but how you dealt with them that mattered! Some people were too quick to give up or take the easy option, but with a bit of thought and stepping out of the situation, it sometimes gives you a clearer picture.

A ferry to Asia

Back on our way, the trusty sat nav on Ginge's bike took us off the main road and into Istanbul! Hmm, I thought, what the hell were we doing? The plan today had been that I got us down into Istanbul, Ginge was going to navigate to the stop off point on the Asian side of the river, and Mike's job was to get us to the hotel afterwards.

Then with Ginge in the lead, after a while we turned into the entrance of a ferry terminal just off the main road. We were near to the blue mosque too! We rode in and enquired where the ferry was going, the chap just smiling at us and was happy to take our money. We really didn't know where we were heading apart from the sat nav had took us there. Anyway, we were on the ferry and this was an adventure - £1 for the bike and rider and it was supposed to take us to Asia, so we thought!

We departed, and to be honest didn't really know where we were actually heading, so the phones came out, even though I'd been told not to turn on the roaming as it was expensive here. I ignored that and got google maps out to see where we were. It was so congested and busy that you couldn't see where Asia was supposed to be when looking across from the harbour. We were on the right track, heading for Üsküdar which was exactly where we wanted to be. In a short 20-25 minute crossing we'd cut out a 2 hour plus ride in congested manic traffic and arrived where we wanted to be for the photo opportunity and champagne. Within minutes of being on the ferry it was time to get off, no timetable just when it was full it left and it was absolutely rammed.

We arrived in Asia, south of Üsküdar, it didn't take long at all. It was mayhem with people trying to get off as quickly as possible. After unloading we decided not to ride out of the port but stopped pretty much where we were and got the bikes ready for happy snaps and video footage.

Our final destination

They were not like in the UK at this port, we were left alone to get on with it, the customs guys even came over to see what we were doing. Some of the police stood by watching us while the cameras were rolling, we popped the champagne open to celebrate our achievement. The police laughed and joked with us but didn't want any champagne, they were happy to have photos taken with us too, although they did stop Ginge from putting the drone up for a few minutes to mark our destination.

After we'd finished and whilst we were sorting out cameras Mike nipped off to buy the return ferry tickets as it would be a huge effort and a little dodgy riding back over the bridge. But whilst he'd gone he was knocked off his bike by a police riot van! They helped him up and made light of it by blaming him, telling him that if he couldn't see their mirrors then they couldn't see him. He shouldn't be riding in their blind spot basically! They Facebooked and WhatsApped the pictures they'd taken of Mike to each other and bought him a coffee whilst we packed away our stuff ready to load on to the waiting ferry.

When we got back on the ferry the bikes all went on together and we soon got chatting to a lovely couple on a Honda Transalp. We discussed lots of things during the 25 minute ferry crossing. It went far too quickly as they were so well travelled and interesting. Ginge said I talked for England and that's why we'd struck up a conversation, but hey, we'd met so many nice and interesting people on this trip so far. They insisted on us returning to Istanbul in the future to meet up with them, so that they could show us around properly. We exchanged details as they were due to visit England in a few months, and we'd drawn up a map and given them places to visit. We docked, said our goodbyes and were off yet again.

Locating the hotel

This time Mike (AKA pathfinder) lead the way, we arrived in the general vicinity of the hotel but ended up riding around and around for about an hour. Things started to get boring and the roads were cobbled, the area was really run down and we were now riding around the Blue Mosque, we must have passed it several times. Eventually after asking some police at a police station that we'd passed, we eventually arrived at the hotel. We got shown where to go and parked the bikes in an underground car park and were given tickets and told we couldn't depart without them.

We unloaded our bikes and headed to the hotel where we were given a warm welcome and our room keys, it wasn't very busy at all. It was a lovely hotel and was cheap because it was suffering from a lack of tourists. It was a 4 star hotel for around €45 a night, bed & breakfast. Showered and changed we met up on the top floor of the hotel. It was just starting to get dark and we had an amazing view of the Blue Mosque and a great vantage point overlooking the city and river towards Asia. We enjoyed a very nice glass of ice cold beer and sat enjoying the fading light and the views as it got dark.

We headed off to dinner, had a couple more beers and discussed the day we'd just had. The restaurant wasn't busy at all, the food was good and we were tired and weary from a long day. It was time for an early night and to get some rest before we headed off tomorrow morning, I wasn't that bothered about staying for any longer than was necessary. Istanbul was busy, dirty and had a bit of a reputation at the moment and the only reason I had come was because it was Ginge's destination, not mine. I'd made the trip '20 Countries in 20 Days' as my goal. This was what Ginge had set out to do and we'd done it, so it was going to be the same routine tomorrow morning, the same as all the other one night stays.

It had been a fantastic day, lots of drama to deal with, lots of new experiences, all adding to the memories of a great adventure. This was a trip of a lifetime and the people in Europe had been brilliant so far. In fact the further East we'd gone, the poorer it had been the friendlier the people had become. I hoped the return leg was going to be just as surprising as the first half.

I don't even remember my head hitting the pillow when I got into bed...

CHAPTER 14

Turkey to Bulgaria

Day 14 - Istanbul to Pleven
(Turkey to Bulgaria)

Date: 19 June 2017
Depart time: 08:30   **Arrive time:** 18:00

Days Mileage: 385 miles
Fuel cost: £28.22 approximately

Route:
Istanbul - Edirne - Plovdiv - Shipka Pass - Pleven

Roads:
It was a tricky start getting out of the small streets in Istanbul before using the motorway to get to Bulgaria. After sorting out the puncture from the day before, we headed north off the motorway, heading for the Passes and twisty roads through the National Park for the rest of the afternoon up to our destination.

Border crossing:
Hundreds of trucks lined the road for 4.5 miles either side of the border. Crossing was very simple, passport and document check before being sent forward to have a bike search that wasn't very thorough.

Weather:
Rain to start with and chilly but brightened up and got warmer as we rode north west.

Countries travelled & Currency:

	Turkish	lira	₺
	Bulgaria	Bulgarian lev	лв

The Days Events - Homeward bound

During the night I'd had to put my ear plugs in to mask the wailing sound outside, which turned out to be calling to prayer. It was really loud and intrusive. I'd also tried to mask the noise from the kids who were running up and down the corridor for what seemed like ages and doors banging in the early hours of the morning. Their parents were very ignorant and had no thought for other people and the fact that they were staying in a hotel that had other people sleeping during the night. Was it kids of today or bad parents of today who are to blame? I certainly thought that the parents are to blame and that they put the onus on other people as to the state of the country and the lack of manners displayed by so many!

Because of the disturbance I was up early and had packed away all my stuff from the night before. I went off to breakfast and met up with Ginge who'd been up on the roof and flown Wander (the drone) for an hour or so earlier, he'd got some great early morning footage from a good vantage point. He told me that Mike had been up for hours and had gone off on his own to the Blue Mosque and a walk around for some happy snaps. I had Mike's spare bike keys, so would have used his bike for the return journey if he hadn't returned. It wouldn't have been very good watching him wearing an orange boiler suit locked up in Syria somewhere. But if that had been the case, then he wouldn't have missed his new BMW GS Adventurer. I could have then borrowed a better bike to continue the rest of the trip and have certainly put the bike through its paces, better than Mike had!

Sorting out a new tyre at a BMW garage in Istanbul

We checked out and headed down to the bikes to make sure everything was ok and load them up. All was in order and we were pretty much ready to go. It was getting really busy outside now as it was Monday morning and people were heading off to work. Ginge had also been to reception and tried to organise a new rear tyre for the journey back but the local BMW dealership said it would take 2 days to get it in and then fit it. We decided we'd head off as the tyre hadn't gone down overnight.

Mike unfortunately arrived back and gave us the rundown of his exploits in Istanbul, he'd wandered around looking like a tourist in the early morning. Probably the only person walking around taking pictures and looking lost! He was approached by a well dressed man in a suit, who spoke very good English and had asked Mike to go with him up some side street to go and look at carpets and rugs! Mike said he seemed like a genuine guy and had considered going with him. Wow, I would have been off like a rat out of an aqueduct, the chap would have seen my ass and a clean set of heels, as I rapidly disappeared down the road. A guy in a suit at 06.00 am in the morning showing his carpets! Come on mate, time to wake up...

Leaving Istanbul

Once we were ready, we gave our car parking tickets to the attendant so that we could leave the car park and were now off into the hustle and bustle of Istanbul's' side roads. It wasn't too bad considering the volume of traffic but we were on a wild goose chase following the sat nav. We were soon on the motorway and travelling back along the same road that we came on, the direction was northeast towards Bulgaria. The route on the motorway was around a 20 mile journey to get to the outskirts of the city. It was said that the population in and around Istanbul was about 20 million, which we could totally understand with the sheer size of the place.

The clouds looked very low, very grey and full of rain. We were not going to be lucky enough to miss this I thought, as we rode towards darker skies (and we weren't). After leaving the city limits, 20 odd miles later it started to rain, a little bit at first and then it came down pretty heavy. We had already pulled in to refuel and made a unanimous decision to put waterproofs on before it had started to pour, but also enroute to the border Ginge had needed to stop. This time to put air in his tyre as it was going down now. It must have been the speed that we were travelling at that had caused it because it had been okay yesterday and had not gone down at all overnight. So we stopped and put more air than is prescribed in the tyre and decided to take it a little easier. If I remember correctly we had inflated it to about 50+ psi. We also took the opportunity to put on more clothing to stop the cold and wet affecting our concentration.

The Turkey to Bulgaria Border

It was a more northerly route that we chose to head to the border. It was a pretty wet and chilly ride out of Turkey, I'd always thought it was hot there but the last couple of days had turned out to be cold and miserable. 150 kilometres later we reached the Turkey/Bulgaria border. It was absolute mayhem, I'd never seen anything like it and probably never will again. There were trucks queued for 4.5 miles either side of the border crossing in both directions.

Litter from the waggon drivers was strewn everywhere, people were walking up and down the line of vehicles selling lots of different things - that may or may not have been useful to the drivers. Cafes and restaurants were also set up on the side of the road to capitalise on the misfortune of the unlucky truck drivers, who must have to wait for hours and hours to be processed through the border. What a mess, I was glad I wasn't driving a truck these days, to get caught up in this kind of nonsense.

Getting out of Turkey was far easier than getting in, although we did have to go through three Turkish border check points first, then riding into 'no man's land' before going through the only Bulgarian checkpoint. It was pretty painless really as they checked our documents and then at the final hurdle they sifted through our panniers! What the hell were we going to smuggle in them when we were this far from home? Anyway, if by ticking a box and by stopping us meant they had done their job then it was no harm done.

A good job they didn't search my side pannier or they would have found an 18 inch machete that I'd packed to use when we were wild camping to chop logs for firewood. We were sent on our way once they'd had enough of seeing our smelly washing and other crap. It had now stopped raining but was still a little cool. I asked the border guard where we could get a new tyre from and he said at the next town which was called Svilengrad.

Riding a motorbike in Bulgaria

As we got through the border and to the other side, the usual photos and videos were taken for the arrival into a new country and then off we went again. The road surface was pretty poor and we were heading for the first town. We'd had to put some more air in the tyre and instead of stopping again at a garage I headed straight into Svilengrad as the border guard had recommended. It was a really run down place, the buildings were derelict and falling apart and people still lived in them.

The roads were really bad too. It was a proper run down place and looked very Russian to me. It was grey and dirty looking and had lots of people that all seemed to be doing the same job. I asked for directions to a garage at the first place we came to. It was a brand new hotel being built and there were lots of guys just hanging around. They didn't understand a word I said, so we moved on. There were four people in the petrol station down the road and three people at the tyre place where we stopped to get sorted out, all doing nothing until we arrived.

As we rode into the petrol station, there happened to be a tyre place at the rear. A guy got up from his chair and came over to us. He didn't speak any English so Ginge said his tyre was 'kaput' in his best German accent, they understood him and were at the bike in seconds. The big shard of metal was pulled out and before we could start filming, he'd inserted the plug, pulled it through, cut it off and checked it had stopped leaking! Wow, that was service for you. He then inflated the tyre to the desired reading and when he was asked about payment, he said 'no.' Ginge didn't accept this and gave the guy a day's wage at least! We decided to stop for fuel and a coffee while we had the chance and as were all sorted out now, ready for another 150 miles or so. We were soon off on our way yet again but only after taking a few pictures of the London cab that was on a plinth next to the garage.

We checked the map too and discussed the next route from where we were and a likely stopping point. It was very ambitious as we didn't know the terrain or what the weather conditions were likely to be in the mountains. Our aim was to get off the motorway, turn right and head north and do the Pass. Then turn left along the mountains before a final right turn heading for the Romanian border. Our destination was Pleven, about 30 miles from the Romanian border.

Riding the Shipka Pass

As we prepared to move off, it stopped raining and almost immediately started to warm up. Our goal was to get to the Beklemeto Pass, that had been recommended by Elena in Greece. Whilst we were so close to the place that she had discussed with me, it would be rude not to go and ride it.

First of all we had to get back on the motorway and get about 100 kms covered before we arrived at our turning. We moved off the motorway and onto a good tarmacked main road. As we approached the turning for the Pass we saw what looked like the golden dome of a mosque in the distance. It was stunning, set in the base of the mountain behind a village. Parts of the village were run down and empty, while other parts looked very new and plush. This was how we would remember Bulgaria. Some places were that run down that they should have been knocked down and in contrast there were brand new buildings, fit for a king.

The landscape was stunning, it reminded me of Snowdonia, only here there were over 400 miles of it. The place was green, very green, there were fields as far as the eye could see, crops, forests, vegetation, mountains, hills, undulating ground, rivers, lakes and streams. This whole place and landscape were beautiful, you would never know this unless you travelled through the country like we were, by getting off the main drag and seeing the real inner country life, for me it was amazing and very pretty.

We headed up the Pass and the views were good as we looked back, not many places to stop but we'd had views similar to this on other mountain passes and mountain ranges in other countries. As we climbed we started heading into cloud base, this was a first and it was getting colder, much colder! Then it started to rain a little, but not enough to worry about, as we headed over the summit and started our descent. It had been raining here too, we'd been lucky to miss this deluge. It was a lovely descent through the forest. Views were limited but we had our eyes on the road, a wet road surface with overhanging trees after a dry spell wasn't the best combination. Getting down in one piece was our only objective. We made it down and the views and scenery didn't disappoint. This country was extremely underrated, it was a pity it was this far away from home as I'm sure it would have been full of bikers, but we hardly saw anyone else for the whole day we were riding!

A lovely lunch in Lovech

After we'd been riding for another hour or so, we found somewhere to stop for a bite to eat. It was around 3 o'clock in the afternoon and we'd not eaten since early this morning, we all felt like we were flagging a little bit. Losing concentration wasn't good, especially when riding in poor weather conditions and on some bad road surfaces. Mike and I had a local dish, consisting of loads of vegetables and some chicken on a hot griddle, which was very healthy and Ginge has some cheese and peppers in batter which wasn't healthy for him. All very lovely and very cheap, €20 for the three of us with drinks and water.

Our bellies were full as we rode off and we soon needed fuel again. This would be the third time today we'd put fuel in the bikes. So it was turning into a long day in the saddle, we had to get some miles in as it was a long way home but we still had plans with plenty to do and see. The views continued to impress and the roads were pretty good in places and then awful in others. Riding one of the roads towards the end of the journey was like being on a trampoline or pogo stick. It was a fast road and the locals did not hang around, no wonder their cars were knackered and looked like they were falling apart. The sheer vibration form hitting potholes would be enough for the tightest nuts and bolts to come loose after a short period of time.

We arrived in Pleven, a little later than planned and a little tired. We headed straight for a hotel and checked in. We hadn't booked anywhere and pretty much stopped at the first place we came across without looking at any other options. As long as it was clean and comfortable, for one night we weren't really that bothered. The City Hotel, Pleven was just a place to grab some rest and be ready to move on again in the morning. We gave ourselves 10 minutes for a beer, this was our usual wind-down for the day and a celebration that we'd got to the end of another day without any major dramas. We then had half an hour or so to shower and change before we wandered down for an evening meal and another cold beer.

A beautiful town in Bulgaria

We met up and walked down towards the town. We took the main road, which obviously wasn't the way to the town square, so we turned left and came across the most beautifully designed set of fountains, amid a very well presented walkway through the town centre. There were bars and restaurants all the way down, open air dining and some really nice looking bars. They weren't very busy but there were lots of people around enjoying the warmth of the early evening. We decided on a place to sit and have a drink and discussed how nice the place was, behind the run down derelict buildings.

The town square was done up really well and could be missed if you didn't go for a walk, as you'd never know it was there. That was one thing we hadn't done everywhere we'd stayed, as we were too tired to bother, but we should've made more of an effort when we were visiting new places.

The place we chose had a bar and restaurant. We weren't really that hungry and decided to have a snack as we'd already eaten late in the afternoon. After dinner, Mike dropped a bombshell and said that he wasn't happy with the way the tour was going. He said he would have preferred more adventure - as in white water rafting, boating and jet skiing. I was a bit taken aback and felt that it was out of the blue. To make matters worse he hadn't really made any effort to organise any routes before we'd set off and rarely took the lead on any days, he could have done some routes while we were away.

The crunch conversation

It wasn't really a heated discussion, but I decided I'd keep out of it because Mike obviously had some issues with something. After all, it was not my trip, I could have dropped out at any time on the lead up to setting off. So I let Ginge deal with it to start with, as he'd organised the tour and I was just tagging on to what he wanted to tick off his bucket list.

Ginge pointed out that Mike had had ample opportunity to get his arse into gear for nearly 3 months, knowing that they were going to Asia. Together they had decided which countries they were going to lead and organise anything they particularly wanted to do. As he hadn't even bothered to look at any routes it was his own fault that we were not doing the things he wanted to now do.

I stayed out of it until I was brought into the conversation, when Mike blamed me for him not doing the routes and said that I'd told him to just 'cuff it' - meaning that he should do it as he went. I didn't hold back any longer and agreed that I had said he would have to 'cuff it' but that was because he had done fuck all towards sorting out the routes we would be taking. Anyway, plans were made in sand for occasions like this and it meant you were pretty free to add things to the itinerary.

I also said that I wasn't happy doing the other adventure activities he was talking about. The trip was enough of an adventure for me, with what I considered great routes, new countries and just dealing with the day to day problems of road closures, map reading errors and just the fact that we were riding anywhere from 120 to 500 miles per day. Besides the trip had taken a different course because of the issues Mike had experienced with riding. He was a little bit out of his depth, he was the weaker rider and everything had really slowed down to compensate for him. He'd had the most issues that we'd taken in our stride and sorted out to ensure he was okay. We'd taken days off the real schedule to get him sorted with his medical issue and now he had the audacity to come out with this!

We kind of agreed to disagree but with hindsight Mike was a new rider to these kind of trips. I did them in a work environment and Ginge did them as often as he could for pleasure. That was the reason we were going to Asia because Ginge had ridden to Africa two years earlier. We headed back to our rooms in good spirits, now that Mike had got something off his chest and we'd all contributed to the conversation and said our bit. We were all tired from the arduous two days riding we'd just had and were ready for bed.

I remembered setting the alarm, it wasn't really needed as we were all wide awake and up before our alarm clocks even went off.

CHAPTER 15

Bulgaria to Romania

Day 15 - Pleven to Corbeni
(Bulgaria to Romania
Transfăgărășan Pass)

Date: 20 June 2017
Depart time: 09:00   **Arrive time:** 18:00

Days Mileage: 170 miles
Fuel cost: £11.92 approximately

Route:
Pleven - Ferry Border crossing - River Danube - Nikopol - Pitesti - Transfăgărășan Pass - Corbeni

Roads:
Great roads all day, some fast sweeping roads to smaller narrow roads through the heart of the country. A very good mix of roads and routes riding north.

Border crossing:
An very unusual border crossing, the border between Bulgaria and Romania is the river Danube. We waited for a ferry and went straight through passport control with ease.

When we arrived at the other side of the river the passport control was very quick, only our passports were checked and then we were charged €4.50 tax per person.

Weather:
Very good, sunny and hot.

Countries travelled & Currency:

	Bulgaria	Bulgarian lev	лв
	România	Romanian leu	lei

The Days Events - Late for breakfast

I'd had a great night's sleep. I was up early writing an account of the previous day for social media. The day started the usual way, up early and start packing stuff away before breakfast around 08:00 am. I was a little bit late arriving for breakfast as Mike and Ginge were already there. They'd already tucked into their food and were enjoying a second coffee. The cooked breakfast was sold as a full English, but it came with cucumber, feta cheese and some other odd bits that we don't have in the UK, it was certainly a 'culinary experience.' Not really that hungry, I ate what I wanted to and left the rest. A good strong coffee was all I needed anyway but when the others had a second coffee it was logged onto their bill. I thought that was very odd!

Discussing and planning the day's route

We had a quick chat about the route for the day and discussed who was leading to start with, who was leading the second bit and who was having the pleasure of the final destination that we'd decided on and popped into our sat navs. The way we'd started to work was for someone to have a town put into their sat nav and the lead bike to run on the cuff by plotting smaller places on theirs. This way we could go off the beaten track but still head in the right direction, if the sat nav had a 'wobbly'. It also meant we had a distance to the next destination, as a reference, so that we could just get straight back to a main road if we needed to, instead of enjoying the off piste experience.

I didn't mind leading the way to the first checkpoint, which was just over the border into Romania, to the beginning of the Pass that we wanted to do. Ginge was leading us up over the Pass as this was on his 'to do' list and Mike had the job of getting us to the days final destination we'd agreed for now. This had a habit of changing, as if we got there early, we'd continue and if it was a bit ambitious we'd stop short and bed down for the night.

Checking out had seemed a bit odd this morning. There'd been a few people just hanging around, going back and forth behind the bar in reception. The lady hadn't spoken very good English but knew that we needed to pay. We'd checked out without any fuss and then loaded the bikes in preparation for the next phase of the journey leaving around 09:00 am (ish). We'd thought it was going to be an easy kind of day, a relaxing ride up to the Transfăgărășan Pass and then start heading towards Budapest, which was on our agenda to visit.

It had been an odd night in Pleven really. It was a run down place until you'd got to the heart of the town, where EU money had transformed it. They'd put a great amount of effort (and money) into the public squares and meeting places.

Riding through northern Bulgaria

Off we went and as we departed noticed that it was quite a busy place, as we negotiated the morning rush hour and the converted electric buses. They were wheeled buses that moved around like any normal bus but as you looked above them, you could see metal framework that was attached to overhead power cables. They were silent, apart from the tyre noise and they had a pretty long lead and manoeuvred through the traffic like any other vehicle. I hoped I didn't meet one face to face again, as I had yesterday, riding the wrong way down the road thinking it was a one way street!

It had taken a while to negotiate our way out of town, because it was quite busy with lots of turns to get to the road we wanted. As we headed out into the countryside it was exactly the same as yesterday. Beautiful views with acres and acres of crops in the fields. Farming was huge here but where did all the money go? It wasn't evident when riding through villages and towns. We couldn't help but slow down to take a look as we passed through lovely landscapes and we all agreed that the scenery was really pretty.

The sat nav took us off the beaten track, we were used to this by now so went along with it but I was always aware of where it was taking us. We headed towards the border and a small town. There was a visible and distinct feeling of poverty here. They didn't have much money at all, the place was fairly run down too.

It was very sad to see, when you moved onto the smaller roads and saw the real country. We saw a young girl who was about 3 or 4 years old in a pushchair, she had black hair and her clothes looked like rags that were wrapped about her tiny frame, with a really dirty, unwashed face. Her eyes had lit up when she'd seen us with a huge smile and she'd waved frantically at Ginge as he rode by. It had pulled on his heart strings and he'd felt like going back to give her a good wash, clean clothes and some money to make sure she was looked after. He had tears in his eyes when he'd relayed the story. Mike and I had already passed before she'd started waving and smiling at us, it was a pity these kids grew up thinking that life like this was normal!

Crossing the Bulgaria to Romanian Border

We started to leave the small town. It had a very wide river on our right hand side, the sat nav told me to turn right. What the hell was it doing I thought! It was directing us into a ferry port! Yep, that's definitely what it had said, I hadn't turned off the 'ferry option' in the settings, so I turned in to stop and speak to the others. "Are we going on a ferry?" Ginge asked, "Just like in Istanbul!" "I don't know" I said. "I didn't know it was here." As it had been sprung on me that morning to lead the first route, I'd had a very quick look at the map and hadn't seen the river Danube as the border crossing. So Ginge took the piss and said that I hadn't planned the day very well (all tongue in cheek of course). This was obviously directed at Mike as a piss take, as he hadn't organised any routes in the few months he'd had to prepare prior to the trip.

A border guard came over and spoke to us in broken English. He was a friendly kind of chap and we established that to get to the Romanian border we had to go by boat but first through customs, when they opened. The next ferry was in 2 hours, so we'd have to wait until the ferry arrived from the other side before our journey could continue. I asked where the closest bridge was, 210 kms was his response, in that direction to the west. I asked about the other direction and he said much further. We decided that we were going to wait for the ferry. It would be over 400 kms if we rode it, just to get to the opposite bank and would take more than a couple of hours.

So, the adventure continued, this had not been expected at all. We really should start to study the maps a little closer in future, but 2 hours passed pretty quickly as we chatted and relaxed. We were first in the queue as we'd been waiting so long, other vehicles had started to join us from around an hour before the boat was due. The ferry/boat was only €2.50 for bike and rider. It wasn't expensive at all being as the river crossing was in the region of 1 km across. It was the widest river I'd ever seen and to be honest you'd easily pay €25 for the privilege of not riding all the way round. After paying we went through customs, I thought that was an odd way to do it but I supposed they had your money first before you were declined at customs!

It was the easiest border we'd been through since the start. The guy only had a quick glance at our passports and gave them straight back, this was the border out of Bulgaria so they weren't too bothered. What would the other side have in store for us? What would happen if we were refused entry? Would we be back on the boat heading back? There would be nowhere to go at that border checkpoint. After all, it was the River Danube that was the actual border and we could hardly just turn around and head off somewhere else to cross. We were sure we wouldn't have any issues but what would they charge a captive audience to get into their country!

Crossing the River Danube by boat

This wasn't a ferry, it was more like a floating pontoon. It was open where you drove on at the back and you drove straight off the front when you landed at the other side. You stayed with your vehicle, in fact inside it if it had 4 wheels or more. We were the first to board and rode down a fairly steep entry slope, over some makeshift steel ramps which made it easier to get onto the boat and up the ramp straight to the front. Then they started loading on the trucks, what a palaver it was. They loaded up by getting the trucks as close together as possible so that they could cram on as many vehicles as they could. Once loaded up we started to head out but then stopped, we saw a vehicle had just arrived at the port, so they went back to shore to collect the articulated truck.

What the hell were they doing we thought, weren't we loaded up enough? We had a very brief chat and a laugh about what was going on. It was certainly an experience and added to our adventure and culture understanding. There was no health and safety here at all. Two chaps were moving the steel ramps around, one was in shorts and a t-shirt with no footwear and the other had a pair of jeans, a t-shirt and some flip flops. The two ramps must have weighed 200 kgs or more and they were dragging them around with a steel rod each.

They moved all the vehicles about as best they could to accommodate this last truck but had overloaded the boat, when they tried to move off they found out it was now grounded! Again they started moving vehicles around in the tight space to enable the boat to tilt and get off the ramp/jetty. They even got us to move our bikes so that a truck behind us could move forward 10 feet or so, other trucks were moved forward too, right up onto the exit ramp. After some major movement they managed to unground the boat until it was moving but they needed to move all the vehicles back before they headed off. So all the trucks were moved backwards until they thought it was stable enough to continue.

We launched and started to head out slowly, very slowly and we were on our way. It was an extremely slow speed and we expected it was well and truly overloaded. We hoped our tour wasn't going to finish at this point and that our bikes didn't end up at the bottom of the River Danube! The guys were running about backwards and forwards with the captain giving his orders. Ginge tried to video the captain and was given a very clear message not to. I supposed he wasn't very happy with the situation of the boat being so weighed down, perhaps he was unsure if it would make it to the other side for the extra €85 they'd made by turning back to collect the last truck.

Going through the Romanian border

Thankfully we arrived at the other side of the river and they beached the boat onto the jetty. We were at the front of the boat and were off first. I videoed the exit as it was extremely lacking in health and safety and I wanted to record us disembarking. I had to put the camera down as I negotiated my exit off the boat after recording Ginge and Mike leaving the makeshift steep ramp that was put up against the boat.

The border guard was great, he spoke really good English and wished us well and a good trip. There was a second checkpoint that Mike had moved to after the customs barrier, the next guy took €4.50 per person from him for entry tax into the country. We were all a little perplexed at what that meant but he paid it anyway and we moved on.

The Romanian flag looked a little sad as it flew on the flagpole, it was extremely well worn and in desperate need of being replaced. We stopped to do our normal routine of flying the Union Flag (Union Jack if on a ship) and took the normal pictures of Ginge and the two of us in a new country. They obviously didn't really care too much about first impressions on entering their country as this place was in a real bad state of repair. It looked really run down and dirty.

As we left the border we rode a couple of miles through the first town, it was a real eye opener to the poverty that consumed this country and its people. A woman was pushing a pram with what looked like huge pieces of driftwood on it, whilst the father carried the child and further on an old lady was dragging a tree that was triple the size of her. She seemed to be in very poor health and was struggling to pull the wood she was trying to move to somewhere, no one helped her, they just walked by getting on with their own business. It was pitiful to watch in the increasing heat but these people obviously did this all the time and literally had nothing. It was just another day for them, doing what they always did but it didn't seem right as we were passing on our journey, doing it for the fun of the tour, riding to Asia and back for pleasure.

As we rode off out of town we were blown away by the beauty of what we saw inland. Crops, rolling hills, agriculture, farmland, people herding goats and cows, lots of horses and donkeys and gaggles of geese everywhere! The countryside was absolutely stunning and not what we expected at all, after our initial introduction at the border and the first town.

There were crops of sunflowers as far as the eye could see. Wheat crops disappearing into the horizon too and as a treat we saw a plane spraying the crops in the distance. The pilot almost gave us an aerobatic display as he banked different ways and did sharp turns whilst dropping spray on the fields of crops. The houses were old and run down. People looked poor and didn't appear to have much to their name. It was proper poverty here but most people waved and looked pleased to see us.

As we headed off the beaten track once again, we saw donkeys and geese for what seemed like every 100 meters or so, horses were tethered up at the side of the road outside people's homes.

Horses and donkeys were used as transport and it was evident as we passed many horse drawn carts that were moving food and other supplies around. Amongst all the poverty we saw top of the range, brand new cars sharing the same roads.

The funeral procession

To our surprise we even stumbled upon a funeral procession, with an open coffin. The body of an old lady was wrapped in cloth but not in a proper coffin as such. The vehicle was like an old van that had the sides cut down and was a low flat bed, less than waist height. The procession was lead by a guy with a trumpet, the priest or vicar was in front of the vehicle with other people too and behind the van was a group of mostly older people with ribbons on their arms. Everyone looked in good spirits as we rode behind them for a few hundred meters until they turned off.

The cars behind had seemed impatient and wanted to get past but there simply was nowhere to go in the very narrow road. What were they going to do, bully their way past or go around on the grass verge! It seemed very bizarre to us but an experience to watch until they crossed a small river and turned left alongside it. They even waved as we went past. We nodded with respect and rode off towards the beautiful scenery ahead.

We had ridden almost 60 miles on really poor roads, it was a long old journey. There were plenty of potholes, lots of poor tarmac and manure everywhere. Taking a good line when cornering was a bit tricky. It had started to become a little bit tedious after a while as we were losing time on top of the earlier delay with the river crossing. But this was the best way to see the real country and we were not in a rush as we didn't have a plan of where we were actually going to stay. There were rivers everywhere and a hive of activity with lots of proper gypsies in old fashioned carts milling around the river in their wooden caravans, not like the skanky tinkers and didicoys you see back home.

We eventually reached good tarmac and headed north towards a town called Curtea de Argeş. Enroute we stopped at the side of the road for what can only be described as very fast food - a plate full of hot chilli peppers, a bowl of pickled veg, about three loaves of bread and two meat kebabs with half a jar of mustard. It was edible but this place was unclean and very rundown, it might have just been the snack bar we'd chosen as others did look better. We really wanted to experience the traditional food that the locals ate but there was a lesson to be learned here for sure!

During our very late lunch we decided to wild camp that evening as the temperature was pretty hot and we felt that it would be nice to camp out at the base of the Mountain Pass. It wasn't that far away and we could stop whenever we saw or found somewhere suitable to camp.

Back on the bikes again we were now heading for the Transfăgărăşan Pass. It was getting late so we stopped at a supermarket for some food supplies for the evening and then headed towards the Pass which was now only about 10 miles away from where we were. The views were amazing as we started to climb, sheer drops on one side and the sheer cliffs of the mountain on the other. If you fell off you'd hit hard rock one way or if you went the other you'd have a long way down before hitting anything! So we took it steady as the roads weren't that good and in places they were still damp from the earlier rain and melting snow from higher up.

Wild bear at the side of the road

As we went around one corner there were two cars stationary, parked at an angle. What the hell's going on here I thought, as I came to an abrupt stop whilst leading and then looked to my left. I saw a bear sat at the side of the road leant up against the crash barrier. I didn't stop for long as I realised it was only about

15 feet away and really wasn't a good place to stop, being so exposed. So I continued past, I didn't want to be hanging around to become dinner!

The guys behind stopped to take some photos and video footage. One of the car drivers was shouting at Ginge but he couldn't understand what was being said. We presumed afterwards that he was telling Ginge not to hang about, as he'd turned off his engine, got his camcorder out and was busy filming.

This was the kind of situation where cameramen could get themselves killed because they were focused on a goal and forgot about the dangers around them as they filmed. Ginge had ignored the shouting and continued videoing until he'd got the footage he wanted. I was busy trying to think of what I could or would do if Ginge had become the bears snack!

I doubted that my machete or axe would've been much use. So I'd decided I'd turn the bike around and ride into the bear had it been necessary. I didn't have a plan after that because my thought process hadn't gone that far ahead. Ginge was safely on the move and out of what could have been a dangerous situation. This had now put paid to our wild camping idea as we didn't want to be woken up in the night by some hungry visitor. Our plan had changed in a nanosecond!

As we set off from our exploits with the wild bear, we came across what looked like a wolf but it turned out to be a wild dog laid in the middle of the road. We stopped and it got up and started running at us in a pretty bad mood, so we lined the bikes up and revved our engines to frighten it out of the way. None of us fancied being bitten by a rabid dog out in the middle of nowhere. It moved to the side of the road pretty quickly and let us pass without chasing us or trying to bite our legs as had happened previously in Croatia.

Stopping before it got too cold and dark

We'd only made it just past the reservoir before we stopped to put on some more layers, as it was getting cold at the base of the mountain. Mike had the best idea that he'd had all day and said "Shall we stop here and see if these cabins do accommodation?" He didn't need to ask us twice after what we'd seen earlier on and as it was getting colder, it was a good call.

We all rode down to a small hamlet of buildings which consisted of hotels, Bed and Breakfast places, boarded up holiday homes and a small church. We found a place for €20 each for the night, which was a huge bonus. It would be warm and dry and without wild bears. It was a must for the evening as it was now pretty chilly too.

There were two bikers from Russia already there, when we rode down to enquire about a room each. When we sat down to have a beer before getting showered and changed, another 6 bikers arrived from Slovakia. The small B&B was probably empty less than an hour ago and now it was bursting with people and all the rooms were taken. A good day for business as it was the first place you arrived at when you dropped down from the main road, - location, location, location.

We had a cold shower as there was no hot water, got changed and headed down for a bite to eat for dinner. We'd bought a huge watermelon and gave it to our host, we said it was for his daughter, he was very grateful for it. We had a chat, downloaded the video footage from the SD cards onto the computer, had another beer and headed off to bed as it had been another long and tiring day.

In the morning we would be fresh and ready for the rest of the Transfăgărăşan Pass, as we were only just at the base of it now.

CHAPTER 16

Romania to Hungary

Day 16 - Corbeni to Budapest via Transfăgărășan Pass (Romania to Hungary)

Date: 21 June 2017
Depart time: 08:30   **Arrive time:** 17:00

Days Mileage: 450 miles
Fuel cost: £49.35 approximately

Route: Corbeni - Transfăgărășan Pass - Timisoara - Arad - Nadlac - Szeged - Budapest

Roads:
A magnificent start to the day on the Mountain Pass and then descended the other side. Some great main roads with plenty of corners and overtaking until lunchtime. We then took the motorway to Budapest.

Border crossing:
A short wait and a quick border crossing showing passports and vehicle documents. Also had to pay for a 'vignette' which is their road tax to ride through Hungary.

Weather:
Hot and sunny, mountains in the morning were chilly with heavy rain and then hot and humid.

Countries travelled & Currency:

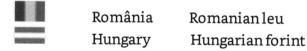

România	Romanian leu	lei
Hungary	Hungarian forint	Ft

The Days Events - Looking forward to the ride

I'd had a great night's sleep, my head had hit the pillow and that had been it until about 07:00 am. I was pretty tired the day before and this was a great place to find as it had been getting on a bit and becoming colder by the hour the evening before. It was a lovely place to stop and relax for the night, even if the bedding was a bit scratchy on the skin (as Ginge had put it). I hadn't noticed, he must have gotten soft in his old age.

Well refreshed, admin sorted out, phones and other electrical items charged up and we were ready to go. We all headed downstairs for a cracking breakfast and a strong coffee. It was really good, a huge omelette with cheese and ham and tomatoes on the side. That was it, I don't think there was a choice as this came out piping hot from the kitchen and it hit the spot just perfectly.

Then our usual routine, back to our rooms and final pack. We loaded the bikes up and paid the bill. We had a quick chat about the day, the weather and what we could expect on the first part of the journey and then got underway.

Our whole stay had cost less than €30 per person. That was for the evening meal, a couple of beers each including bed and breakfast. Before we left we'd talked to some of the Slovakian riders. One had spoken English really well so we'd asked him for some good routes that we could do during our trip through Slovakia. They gladly obliged after a big discussion amongst themselves, which we couldn't understand and came up with a few routes of where we should and must ride when we were there.

They too, along with the other few bikers, were getting ready to depart. We were the only ones that were heading up the Pass as they'd come from that direction the night before. It was funny really, bikers had their own little individual routines to get ready for the day and we were all no exception.

Riding the Transfăgărăşan Pass

We were now ready for our journey and were half prepared for the day in Slovakia too - thanks to our Slovakian friends. We said our goodbyes and wished each other a safe and good trip ahead, then departed ready to head off up the Pass. It wasn't long before we reached good views. In fact it was almost immediately. As we turned the next few corners, the roads were getting twisty as we climbed. Unfortunately the surface wasn't that great, it was in bad need of repair from the hard winter.

We spoke to some other bikers and they told us that today was the fifth day the Pass had been open. No wonder there weren't many bikers on it ,as it usually stayed closed until 01 July because of the weather conditions. It was a stroke of luck then for us that it was open and ready for our arrival at this early stage in the season. Otherwise it would have only been possible to go so far and then we would have had to turn back, as we'd found out when we were going through Slovenia some days earlier. An old Army saying that we used to say was - 'I hate backtracking!'

We stopped several times enroute to the top to take lots of photos. Sometimes stopping alone, other times as a pair or group because the scenery was absolutely stunning. I moved on ahead and found a really good vantage point high up, so that I could get the DSLR camera out and take some 'zoomed in' good pictures of the other two climbing the Pass far below from where I was and some better video footage and close ups. It was really hard to take in the whole view and store it in the grey matter and personal memory bank.

Where did you look first at such a magnificent place? It reminded me of the Rockies in Canada. The whole place was still thawing out in mid June. They'd obviously had a lot of snow that had caused many problems on the roads and for people transiting the mountain. I'd hate to have to find a way around this Pass if it was closed.

On top of the world

We reached the top of the Pass as a trio. It wasn't the summit but it was high enough. There was a pile of snow cut away from the road that was at least 12 foot high. A couple of German bikers came out of a tunnel and stopped to tell us that it was still very cold in there and very slippery. As we headed through the 100 metre or so tunnel we didn't have any issues and when we reached the other side, WOW!

It was a beautiful sight looking down the really deep valley out onto the flat plains miles below, some 10-15 kms away in the distance, or maybe more. Stunning, absolutely stunning, so of course we stopped for more pictures. Ginge launched 'Wander' (the drone) and we took even more pictures of the twists and curves below. I'd rather ride up this side than down it as it looked awesome - ask any biker about riding a Mountain Pass and they'll tell you that they'd rather climb than descend.

The views were amazing, the road wasn't the best because of its condition, but we got a bit of pace up as we went. At the bottom it was photo time again, this was why places like this took so long to negotiate. You had to savour every moment of the views and record your presence for later memories. Mike bumbled down at the back as he'd enjoyed this Pass tremendously, even though he hadn't been looking forward to it beforehand.

Onto the flatter section, the roads improved and were enjoyable to ride, very twisty and with some decent corners. This didn't last for very long though as we needed to get some bigger miles in and the motorway was our chosen route. We got to the motorway pretty quickly and turned left. We travelled west now with the mountain range on our right. It was well off in the distance but a wonderful sight. To the left and right hand side were fields and fields of crops. It was amazing how much farming was still done by hand and most farms had horse and carts, people in fields tending to crops and also shepherds in the middle of nowhere with sheep, cattle and goats.

As we rode with the mountains on the left, we came back down to low level and then there was a new set of mountains on the right, the same land featured but in reverse. The little towns and villages looked really quaint in the distance either side of the motorway, there were between 100-200 houses and looked really pretty with their backdrops of beautiful scenery. The motorway spoilt it, as it had been carved straight through the middle of natural beauty, rolling hills and green fields and lots of them. On the right hand side was a feature that reminded me of Ayers Rock in Australia, I'd only seen pictures of it but it just stood out prominently as we rode towards and then past it.

Never trust a sat nav over a map

The mountain grew and was now ahead of us too, we sort of meandered our way to the left of it and the motorway came to an end. We then left the motorway and headed towards Arad on some really nice twisty roads, this section was quite fast but also congested. We were only about 50 miles away from Arad and Ginge came up next to me and said we'd missed the turn, but my sat nav had said straight on and upon looking at the map it was the most direct route.

Mike confirmed the left turn on his sat nav and as it was 'democracy rules' (2 against 1) we turned around and went back to the last turn they reckoned I should have taken 'I still hate backtracking'. To top it all they blindly followed directions without knowing where we were. I didn't purchase £80 worth of maps for nothing before the trip, I liked to know where I was, where I was going and what roads I was using. Anyway, I sat at the back with my arse in my hand and let the democracy pair of sat nav wankers lead for a few hours!

This was going to add a good couple of hours to the journey. I was happy riding for long periods of time and didn't mind the extra miles but this was going to take us straight onto the motorway. I could see on the map what the sat nav was trying to do and we were heading due south instead of north. Mike missed the motorway signs and headed off down a smaller road, so I had to jump in and say something. "We are heading in the wrong direction" I told Mike "We should be going north not south."

He didn't have a clue, he had merrily followed the sat nav, blindly ignorant of where we were, where we were going and how we were going to get there! There were better roads we could have been using, so we turned around again and headed to the motorway that we'd passed a mile or two ago. It was brand new and not on any sat navs yet! Going off route though we'd found an aeroplane in somebody's front garden, what the hell was that all about! We took some pictures, turned around and headed for the motorway once again, Mike decided he wasn't leading anymore. So it was his turn to throw his teddy out of the pram, even though he'd instigated the earlier U turn as his sat nav had instructed him to go off the route. I had decided to stop them, so I went back in front until we were back on track within a mile or so.

This time we were going to be travelling on the motorway until we reached Budapest. We'd have a few breaks enroute to fill up and also a chance to stop at the border. We'd got around 450-500 miles to travel depending on the route taken, it was a big mileage day and something that had to be done sometimes. We all hated it but it was a necessary evil, to crank some miles in and get on with it on the motorway.

As we headed further west, the villages and small towns got bigger. There was definitely more money around here but the brand new motorway was nearly empty. It reminded me of the M40 when it was first built and nobody used it. The landscape had now started to get flatter and it was getting hotter by the minute. As we rode we could feel a wall of heat as if someone had just turned up the heating a few notches.

We had managed three fuel stops and even as we sat in the shade when we stopped, it was uncomfortable. After taking on fluids and a bit of fuel for our bodies, we were off again, sometimes with a welcome ice-cream to cool down. It didn't work for long but tasted nice and made us feel better whilst we were chomping on cold ice cream.

Crossing the Romania to Hungary border

Then we reached the border and were surprised that it was a pretty well set up border control. It was only a short wait and then we were through by showing passports and vehicle documents. We had to stop in the slip lane just after the border and pay for a 'vignette' which was a type of road tax to ride through Hungary.

The normal stop ensued to take pictures and a short video and the Union flag came out to show a new country for Ginge. It was a nice little routine, got us off the bikes and gave us a bit of bonding and social time too. Riding this many miles was quite solitary at times as you were left with your own thoughts for miles and miles at a time. It gave you head space though, thinking time and a chance to reflect on life.

Onwards to Budapest after our brief stop and payment at the booth. It was a boring journey but the fun hadn't started yet. The landscape became ultra flat, somewhat like Holland but it stretched out for miles in either direction. It was arable too and had lots of different crops, predominantly wheat, corn and sunflowers.

A huge storm as we rode towards Budapest

Then, in the distance we saw a huge black cloud, and we were heading straight for it. It was big, very, very big. We weren't going to avoid it as we were heading straight towards the middle. The wind picked up and the rain started, we pulled over and put our waterproofs on. It was still hot and humid but as we got closer the wind picked up even more and the rain was a welcome respite from the heat. It cooled down to about 15-20 degrees, which was lovely and refreshing. But the wind was blowing us all over the road and our visibility was now drastically reduced.

We dropped our speed down to about 50 mph, which in hindsight was still a little bit too fast for the conditions, but then by sheer coincidence, as the lightning flashed all around us, there was a gap in the clouds directly in front of us. There were two storms, the one on the right, which was huge, and the one on the left, which was its baby sister, luckily we were headed straight between them and it cleared up pretty quickly.

The temperature rose once again and it was sweltering, back up to 35 degrees in a matter of minutes. We only had 20 miles to go to get to our destination and then it would be time to find a hotel. With an Ibis hotel programmed into the sat nav we headed to the city centre. The hotel was full as expected, so it was a good job we had booking.com on our phones as we found another place a few miles away. We headed there, it was clean, cheap and cheerful and okay for one night. We checked in, unloaded our bikes and went off to the rooms. They offered us remote controls for the TV at an extra cost but we left them on the counter as we wouldn't be needing them.

Our plan was to have a shower, get changed and head straight into town for a bite to eat and a well deserved beer, not to sit in the hotel room watching television that we wouldn't be able to understand. The taxi was ordered when Mike got down to the reception, Ginge and I were not too far behind him and by the time we'd got downstairs the taxi arrived and we were on our way. We asked the taxi driver to take us to the centre where the restaurants and bars were as we didn't want to be wandering around this late playing 'find somewhere to eat.'

A bikers night in Budapest

We arrived and the place was buzzing with lots of people enjoying the warm summer evening. We had a little walk around to find somewhere suitable to eat before agreeing that we should stop and have a beer to start with. Beer in hand and a few glasses of water, as we were all dehydrated, we were happy once again, but still hot and sweaty. Our damp kit was drying out in our hotel rooms and right now life could not have been better. We were sat in Budapest with a cold beer watching the world go by, just perfect.

We found a nice looking restaurant that wasn't selling the usual burgers and chips and sat down to a really nice Hungarian meal. It was traditional goulash with some side dishes and tasted absolutely divine. The flavours were mouth watering and were washed down with a glass or two of beer and a jug of water. We sat and watched the place get busier by the minute and before long we were ready to head back to the hotel. It had been a long hot day and we were drained and ready for bed.

Could three become two!

When we arrived back at the hotel, Mike dropped a bombshell and said that he might be heading home the next day, as he had lots going on and needed to get back. We kind of half expected it, as he'd already said he wasn't interested in going to Berlin but we hadn't expected it at that precise moment in time. Anyway we sort of said our goodbyes but would have a proper farewell over breakfast the next morning. Tired and weary we went off to bed wondering what tomorrow would bring and whether Mike would stay with us for a few more days.

Could it be down to just two riders tomorrow morning?

CHAPTER 17

Hungary to Czech Republic

Day 17 - Budapest to Ostrava (Hungary to Czech Republic via Slovakia)

Date: 22 June 2017
Depart time: 08:30   **Arrive time:** 18:00

Days Mileage: 340 miles
Fuel cost: £39.30 approximately

Route:
Budapest - Vac - Šahy (Slovakia) - Lučenec - Brezno - Banská - Žilina - Čadca - Trinec (Czech Republic) - Ostrava

Roads:
A fantastic day, riding all sorts of roads. Fast twisty mountain and B roads with some good overtaking. The scenery was great when riding through the gorges and alongside rivers - just brilliant.

Border crossing:
An open border for both Hungary to Slovakia and Slovakia to the Czech Republic. There were old border crossings for both countries but they were not manned.

Weather:
Very hot and humid, up to 36 degrees. Cooler in the mountains in Slovakia.

Countries travelled & Currency:

	Hungary	Hungarian forint	Ft
	Slovakia	Euro	€
	Czech Republic	Czech koruna	Kč

The Days Events - And then there were two

At around 05:00 am I heard a bike start up a couple of times. It was the sound of a BMW R1200GS and the second time it started up it rode off. There was no mistaking, it was Mike's bike, he'd said he'd be off the night before, unless of course the bike had been stolen. I didn't need to look at the clock but knew it was early as Mike was an early riser. He'd said he had some pressing personal matters that he had to attend to. So now the trio of riders became a duo.

It was a great pity that he wasn't able to see the tour out to the very end as it was always nice to finish what you'd set out to do. We had tentatively wished him well the previous night just in case he was up and off early. We hadn't really expected to see him at breakfast as he'd made his mind up.

He'd already made a few comments about not wanting to go to Budapest, as he'd been there several times before and said that he didn't want to finish the tour in Berlin, as he'd also been there and done that too. He'd looked on the map and said how much further it was going to be riding further north, instead of heading home!

Ginge sent me an early text message saying that he'd also heard the bike start up and ride off and had inquisitively got up to find Mike's room empty with him already gone. We had an early rendezvous to discuss the day's events, now that it was just the two of us. We decided that we wouldn't stay in Budapest (as previously planned) for the day, as we were not there to sightsee and there was a fantastic route that we'd been given in Slovakia.

Together we could do some big mileage and explore the roads a bit easier as a pair. Mike's riding had been okay for him, with the experience he had but he wasn't at the same level as Ginge and I. So we would make much better time and do more miles each day from now on, now that he'd gone. It would be much easier too as we'd kind of nursed him along for the majority of the trip and slowed the pace right down to accommodate his riding ability.

Anyway, neither of us were perturbed about it and with spirits still very high we got up as normal, packed our belongings after a shower and started on the road around 08.00 am. We had already discussed the route to the Slovakian border and got underway. The idea was to get to the border before stopping for a coffee and bite to eat for breakfast, as we hadn't had any breakfast booked at the hotel. But sat navs being sat navs, they decided to recalculate at a critical turning point and we went into a service station, which was just before the turning that we'd wanted.

It had looked as though the road went out the other side of the services and probably did,but we saw a McDonald's and stopped straight away for breakfast and a coffee. Ginge went to get the breakfast and there was a coffee shop in the same building, so I headed over to get some extra large coffees to get us wide awake for the day ahead.

Crossing the Hungary to Slovakia border on a motorbike

The route for the day was finalised over our 'cardboard breakfast', whilst we drank the biggest cup of coffee I'd ever had. After ablutions we headed north on the main road, which took us straight to the Slovakian border. The roads were great, big twisty corners going up and down hill.

The border crossing was very good too with no issues or problems, so we took the opportunity to do the normal picture and video routine. It was a must for Ginge and I'd grown to enjoy it too. As there was only two of us a guy who was sat in his truck jumped out and offered to take a picture of us both with the flag.

When we were on the Transfăgărăşan Pass, we'd bumped into a group of Slovakian riders and asked them where we should ride in Slovakia. They'd told us two areas that we should visit but warned us that the roads weren't good but the GS was made for these roads. There was an area to the south that we should ride and one further north above half way into the country but a little further east of the route that we really wanted to take.

We needed to be heading north west for the next border but it would have been a really easy hour and a half transit through Slovakia and we would have missed the opportunity to see the country properly. So we decided to take the longer more demanding route and headed in a different direction and turned due East.

It had to be fun or it wasn't worth doing! Initially the road was pretty good but at times it lived up to expectations and was very bad. The road surface and potholes were awful and sometimes it felt like it would shake the bike to pieces, the going was pretty slow because of the poor roads.

Breathtaking scenery in Slovakia

The countryside was amazing and very beautiful. It had it all as we slowed down to take in the scenery. We rode through pine forests, where you could just glimpse open fields that were dotted about. The roads went up and down but you couldn't see much with the dense forest all around and it smelt lovely as we rode through the cool vegetation. Then it started to open up and the land was rich in crops and undulating fields. The landscape was awesome with small villages and very small towns nestled into the hills. The churches were splendid too and we expected that they were a focal point for the locals because of all their splendour. We weren't sure of the religion but they seemed wealthy, well kept and brand new.

After a couple of hours we stopped for a quick ice-cream and checked on our progress and the next phase. The town we stopped in was very clean and the children that were around seemed well dressed and friendly. The plan was that we'd head towards the mountains next and have some lunch there in an hour or so when we started to feel hungry. The roads were fabulous, empty in the most part but a bit bumpy in places.

The landscape reminded me of Bavaria and Austria, and when we were in the mountains it had a definite Alpine feel to it, twisty roads with steep sides and if you went over the edge it was going to be a long way down. This country had snow in the winter and lots of it, the houses had steep rooftops which I assumed would stop the snow from getting too deep and heavy on the roof but what did I know, I was just guessing!

We decided to go for a play on the twisty roads and saw mountains that were covered in trees, areas that showed signs of avalanches the previous winter, and there were ski lifts, rivers and lakes. All the nicer looking areas were lined with houses and places to stop. I was sure it was a tourist destination for many people but not familiar to us Brits. You could also park anywhere you liked and didn't get charged or ripped off for it, like you would in 'Rip off Britain.' It certainly was a lovely part of the world and I was pleasantly surprised as we rode through some fantastic places that we hadn't expected to ride.

We stopped for fuel when we were almost empty as there weren't that many garages around out in the sticks and stumbled across a garage around lunchtime. We also had a bite to eat for lunch, and as we weren't that hungry decided on just a sandwich and a drink before we headed for the Czech Republic border. It was still some distance away and we wouldn't get there until at least 5:00 pm. Enroute we found some great fast roads and we certainly took full advantage of them.

It was much quicker with just two of us and we had a nice little routine going on, taking it in turns leading and map reading (well I used the map, Ginge used his sat nav) but this time we didn't have any map reading or route selection hiccups and even if we did we were having a lot of fun. A few extra miles would certainly have been a bonus.

Crossing the Czech Republic border on a motorbike

We followed a magnificent river for what seemed like ages, as we headed towards the border. There were people rafting and boating on it and with the mountains as a backdrop it looked picture perfect. We weren't hanging around though as we meandered our way on the light grey tarmacked road, adjacent to the vivid blue river, lined with deep green vegetation.

The traffic started to get really heavy and busy so we filtered for at least half an hour as we approached the border. The terrain started to level out and we knew we'd be leaving Slovakia behind very soon, the border drew closer by the minute. We reached an unmanned border taking us into the Czech Republic, in fact we had to turn around and go back to the borderline for pictures and filming as we'd sailed by without realising we had crossed the actual border.

We had a quick chat about the next section of riding and decided that we were going to head north for 30 miles or so. We could reach Poland tonight if we wanted to but what was the point in not experiencing this country first. Besides we hadn't got any plans except to stop for fuel when we were empty, food when we were hungry and for the night when we'd had enough or were tired.

We rode north, the area was very clean and tidy, people were dressed pretty well, gardens and buildings were well kept and maintained. The houses had their own bit of land that you could clearly see and it was nice that they didn't barricade themselves in like we did back home with big fences and trees lining their boundaries.

We went through a built up area and Ginge looked at the sat nav for local hotels. This proved to be a big mistake, trusting one of those things again after the problems they'd caused! Everywhere looked pretty poor to be honest and very run down, my initial thought was washed away at how nice it had looked. Ginge led us straight to a derelict block of flats that looked like they were ready to be demolished, it was once a hotel as the sign suggested but I would not have stayed there anyway.

It looked like a real rough place, the only thing missing were the drug addicts and used needles lying around. We had a laugh at the situation that we were in, sat outside a real dive that was disused and run down and wondered when the sat nav had last been updated properly. We took a few pictures before departing so that we could remember this in years to come. Afterwards we were in search of a proper town to stay in. Once again we were on the move, this time towards Ostrava.

Finding digs in Ostrava

The roads enroute to Ostrava were pretty good, the speed limits were fairly low and people drove like they had all day. They were not in a rush at all, or were the fines that heavy for speeding that people didn't want to get done for going over the speed limit? We eventually reached Ostrava, a bit later than planned and without reservations for anywhere to stay. We found a couple of hotels from looking online, one was very expensive and only had very small rooms so we didn't stay there and the other was less than half the price and looked clean, so we chose it. It was only a place to safely put our kit for the night, sleep for an evening and go through the same routine again in the morning, that we'd become accustomed to.

The hotel was situated in the heart of a busy street where it was all happening with bars, restaurants and lots of people. As we rode up we found that we could park directly in front of the hotel. We checked in and then ventured across the road and sat down for a quick beer before getting a shower. Watching the world go by was a nice way to relax as we started to unwind and reflect on the last 24 hours. It had been a great day and we'd covered lots of pretty fast miles as a pair. We went for a nice meal after our welcome beer and shower, there were some lovely looking ladies around and the guys all looked like they worked out in the gym. We deduced it was because competition was high, that they needed to blow their chests up to impress to get the best girl.

It was a strange night out really because everyone seemed to be into smoking from a glass bottle, with fruit in the jar - which seemed pretty odd to me. Groups of guys all sat around a table with beers passing around a peace pipe. Even tables with just females on them had the same thing but in different colours and flavours. It was a really busy place and there were loads of people enjoying the warm evening at the many bars and restaurants that lined this particular street. It was going to be noisy tonight, so the window would be closed and ear plugs in when I drifted off to sleep later on.

Our bellies were now full of good food, we rehydrated ourselves with a litre of water each and a small beer. It was now time for bed as we hadn't slept very well the night before and it had been a great day's riding, which always tired you out.

The weather was still very hot and humid, it was cloudy and the place was green. I expected there would be some rain in the night as it felt like the heavens would open but who cared we were not camping tonight. As we strolled the 100 meters back to the hotel, we said goodnight to each other and arranged breakfast for 08:00 am the next morning.

I don't remember falling asleep as I sank into a very comfortable bed with a light duvet and my ear plugs in.

CHAPTER 18

Czech Republic to Germany (Auschwitz)

Day 18 - Ostrava to Dresden
(CZECH REPUBLIC to
GERMANY via POLAND)

Date: 23 June 2017
Depart time: 08:00   **Arrive time:** 21:30

Days Mileage: 360 miles
Fuel cost: £14.68 approximately

Route:
Ostrava - Zory (Poland) - Auschwitz - Katowice - Wrocław - Bautzen (Germany) - Dresden

Roads:
Started off on the motorway to get to our first stop quickly, had a short time on normal roads to get to Auschwitz. After our stop we used the motorway to crunch in the rest of the miles.

Border crossing:
Open borders, straight through without slowing down or stopping on the motorway going from the Czech Republic to Poland. Exactly the same riding from Poland into Germany.

Weather:
Weather was warm and humid with rain threatening, turned cooler early evening in Germany.

Countries travelled & Currency:

	Czech Republic	Czech koruna	Kč
	Poland	Polish zloty	zł
	Germany	Euro	€

The Days Events - A breakfast surprise

I woke up with a start after hearing huge claps of thunder. Even with my ear plugs in it was loud, the rain was heavy and hammering on the window. A huge thunderstorm stayed around for a while, with lots of thunder and lightning which lit up my dark room. My earplugs made it seem like it was further away than it actually was and off somewhere in the distance. Although a big clap of thunder must have been overhead because it was so loud and had woken me up. It hadn't affected a good sleep though, as I must have drifted back off once I'd gathered my thoughts and realised it was only a slight disturbance and nothing too sinister.

The day started exactly the same way as any other, up, showered and things packed away before going to breakfast. We'd arranged an 08:00 am start for breakfast with maps and iPads to organise our day. We had a really nice breakfast with a choice of hot or cold food (or both) and as much coffee as we wanted. As we sat discussing our day a lovely waitress attended to our table. She was a young and a very attractive lady who engaged with us about our trip.

She spoke perfect English and we laughed and chatted about our lives, where we came from and what we'd been doing. She'd worked on a cruise ship for a number of years and the common language had been English. It was a really pleasant conversation and we wished each other well before Ginge and I departed with full bellies once again.

We headed back to our rooms and packed our remaining kit, then went down to reception to check-out. The bikes were very quickly loaded and ready for the day and we departed once again. There was only the two of us now so things were a little slicker and a bit quicker for us to get underway.

Crossing the Czech Republic to Poland border

Loaded up and ready to go, with plenty of fuel in our tanks from the previous day we put Auschwitz into the sat nav for the quickest route. It took us straight onto the motorway without any views. We wanted to spend some time in Auschwitz and were keen to get there as early as possible, it wasn't too long before we were crossing the border into Poland. The border was just a sign and if you blinked you would have missed it. We didn't fancy stopping on the motorway, so the photos would have to wait until we arrived in Auschwitz. The houses in Poland were very nice, very unique in shape, size and colour with an old German/Austrian feel about them.

The beautiful countryside was clean and well kept. Enroute to Auschwitz there were flat open fields full of crops with mountain ranges flanking us way off in the distance on the right hand side. Because of the direction we were now travelling, it was possible that this could be the range of mountains we'd ridden in Slovakia the day before.

Auschwitz concentration/death camp

Personally, I had been looking forward to this day from the very beginning of the tour, as it was on my bucket list of things to do. Silent in thought whilst riding gave many hours of headspace but today was different. I imagined all those years ago, in the early 1940's, people making the very same journey that we were now but they, not knowing their own fate. They were led the same way, seeing the same pretty views.

Our riding journey was nearing an end as we were in the final stages of our three week tour. But for the millions of poor, unsuspecting people who had done this very same route, all those years ago, it was to be the end of their life. It was quite an emotional journey for me as we rode towards our first destination of the day. As we approached the gates of Auschwitz, it became even more surreal, knowing what carnage had happened here for many years and to so many people.

We arrived at the main camp and with military precision were directed to parking spaces. We were well looked after and shown to a very small area near the gates, where the bikes would be in full view of the parking attendants. We both felt it was a safe spot to leave them as we couldn't carry all our belongings around with us.

Ticket collection was next and we were given a time to watch a film and then straight afterwards a time for a guided tour in English. We were not sure if you could go it alone but being guided on each section of this terrible place would give us more detailed information about it. Being ex military men, we knew the need to have a better understanding of the atrocities that really happened here.

We had to go through security before our designated time to watch the short film. Ginge had his 'man bag' full of bits and pieces with him as he'd wanted to carry some valuables instead of leaving everything on his bike, but he was stopped and told he couldn't take his flag through at this point. There was no explanation, just that he had to get rid of it before going on. I was already through security, so Ginge took his flag back to the bike, I waited for him before we entered the small cinema and watched the film. After that we waited outside for our English speaking guide to show us around the first part of Auschwitz.

A sorrowful end to human life

As we were led around to different parts of the concentration camp, it was despicable what had happened here for so many years. It was totally unbelievable to think that human beings could do this to one another. Young men, young women, children, old men, old women and everyone in between, all herded into areas like cattle and either killed by gassing or worked to death, depending on which line they were sent.

It was an emotional tour for myself and Ginge. Just taking a step back after seeing all of it made you realise just how big it was and some people still think it never happened. How could they be so short sighted, narrow minded and blind, It truly beggars belief!

In the safety of well preserved buildings, protected behind glass for visitors to see, were tonnes and tonnes of human hair, piles of spectacles, gold teeth extracted from the dead, adult clothes, baby clothes, shoes, suitcases, combs and valuables. They had, at the last stage of their lives, been stripped of their final belongings, so close to the end of their lives with nothing left to give. Then in a barbaric and inhumane way, had their final breath of life taken away from them once they'd been deprived of their very last belongings and then their dignity.

It was a very calculated process, cunning and underhanded. The Germans knew exactly what to do to make this process more efficient and more importantly to hide it from the rest of the world. The labour parties of workers, who'd been chosen to do the work of murdering hundreds of thousands of people and undertook the unbelievable task of gassing people and burning their bodies, also lost their lives after 3 months of hard labour. This ensured it got rid of the people who knew what was really happening. They destroyed every shred of evidence to conceal their evil!

We were allowed to take photos in almost every part of the two camps that we'd visited. I didn't take any pictures when we got to the room where the children were on display, as a mark of my respect. It didn't seem fitting or right to have pictures on my phone or SD card of young children who were used in barbaric experimental procedures for my own keepsake and mementos, as others in the group were doing. That memory would be etched in my mind for the rest of my life and not on a keepsake photograph taken by me.

Auschwitz Birkenau 2 - Concentration/death camp

We left Auschwitz with silent thoughts. There was no need to discuss what we'd seen there, as it was obvious how everyone felt with the sombre mood that seemed to engulf us all. As we wandered out of the camp to where we'd started the tour, we were told that the next part would start in half an hour or so. We headed off for a quick comfort break and something to eat, but when we arrived back the group must have met early and left. So we had a decision to make, would we go to Auschwitz - Birkenau or leave?

We decided to stay as we really did want to experience the whole place, as it could be our last visit, you didn't know with these kind of things. Once it had been seen, would you ever want to do it again or was there too much to take in properly, that a second visit would be needed.

We found a bus that was taking groups to the next location and got on it. We drove down the same road that we'd ridden that morning, and had actually passed Birkenau without knowing what it was. When we arrived we went in and tried to find our group but there were thousands of people there all milling about, wandering here, there and everywhere.

This camp was huge, there was no mistaking that it was where the larger part of the exterminations had taken place. It was a massive open expanse of land with barbed wire fences all around, and because of its scale it would have housed many thousands of people. The main railway track came directly into the centre of the camp and was an eerie setting, with the low cloud base and drizzle that had started to fall.

Many buildings were demolished or rotten as they were wooden huts in the main. They'd housed hundreds of people in appalling conditions before they had been worked to death or killed because of their background. It was such a shock to see and envisage, actually being here, even though you knew what had happened and had seen the photographs and documentaries.

It was so overpowering when you started to grasp the sheer size of the operation that was concocted by evil men. We eventually found our group after we'd had a look around, we stayed with them for the remaining hour or so of the tour. The guide was brilliant with her knowledge and delivery of information and she brought the place back to life in a very sobering and respectful way.

A respectful departure

Our extremely moving tour came to an end 6 hours after we'd arrived. We reflected that people had lost their lives here in the most terrible way, in order for us to have a future and the freedom that we now enjoyed.

We had pictures of Poland to take for the usual flag routine. As a fitting end we decided to go outside of the camp gates with the flag to show our respect and honour to those who gave their lives for us. We got ready for the next phase of our journey, as we were lucky enough to have the ability to finish our adventure - whilst so many didn't get that chance to finish theirs over 70 years ago.

After taking more photos and repacking some of our kit, we took a comfort break before departing. Leaving Poland we took the main roads and motorways, as we had 200 kms to ride before we'd arrive in Germany. We headed straight there on a direct route as our aim was to get to Colditz, maybe we'd make it by the evening, it was a long way and quite late, as it was 17:30 pm before we actually left. We had toll roads and motorways programmed into the sat nav so that we didn't have to map read and took the fastest roads straight there without deviating.

The motorways were boring but sometimes very necessary, especially when it was late and you had big miles to crunch. The roads through Poland were flat and full of crops being grown either side of the motorway, farming was very big here too. This time on a proper agricultural scale, the fields didn't have horse and carts like so many poorer places we visited and witnessed in days gone by. Life was certainly richer in these parts for so many, but were they as happy as most of the poorer people we'd come in contact with on our journey?

They certainly didn't look like it, as they passed us in the 'hurry of life' at well over 100 miles an hour, like we were stood still and we weren't hanging around travelling at 90 mph! It just reminded me of back home now, millions of ants going about their own daily business without integrating or taking any notice of what was going on around them, as they were in their own little world.

Enroute we witnessed over 15 miles of pine forest as far as the eye could see on either side of the motorway. The smell was unbelievable and refreshing. We were getting closer to the border for Germany and there were rows and rows of wind turbines. Back to our world and the rat race of life I thought with a heavy heart, do I really want to step back into this?

Crossing the Poland to Germany border

A full tank of fuel from when we left our starting point, with a stop when we were almost empty, meant almost two tanks of fuel later we were tired and a little drained, we decided to stop in Dresden. I'd played fuel roulette a few times during this trip and breaking down on the motorway, without enough fuel would not be happening here. I was reading less than 30 miles on the clock, so continuing any further would be stupid.

We looked for an Autohof, which was a place for truck drivers to stay. They had petrol stations, places to stay and decent food at reasonable prices. They'd sprung up over the years to allow truck drivers to get off the motorway and go straight to a place to stop overnight, rather than congest the local infrastructure by parking anywhere at the end of their driving hours. When we arrived, we filled up and ate as it was now around 9:00 pm and we'd been at it non stop after a long day. The accommodation was full so we couldn't stop there. The food was good and we headed off to find a hotel just around the corner, positioned on the River Elbe not far from the town centre and Autohof.

We found the Mercure hotel with ease as it was just over the river and was very nice too. It had to be really, as it was going to be our last hotel stay on this adventure. Ginge enquired about a couple of rooms in his best German while I waited outside in case they couldn't accommodate us.

There were plenty of hotels around as it was a real touristy place but neither Ginge or I had ever visited before. It wasn't long before he returned and said we could park in the underground car park which was situated around the back. It was secure and locked at night so our bikes would be safe, even with all the luggage left on them.

A splendid hotel to finish the tour

We parked up and unloaded only some of our gear, as it was gated parking and nobody was getting in or out without being watched. We grabbed the stuff we needed and before we did anything else we had a ritual beer and celebrated getting back into homeland for Ginge. We toasted our final night in a nice hotel before riding to Colditz in the morning. That was now our final plan as we were originally going to finish in Berlin for a picture at the Brandenburg Gates. It wasn't long before the strong german beer took effect on our tired bodies, we were ready for a good night's sleep and we really wanted an early start.

We both retired to our respected rooms with just our wash bags from our luggage as we were only there to sleep, I got a quick shower and then went straight to bed. The white noise was still ringing in my ears from the fast motorway miles and I had not yet settled down, still full of adrenalin and still wide awake it would take some time to get off to sleep.

As I lay there I reflected on what had happened so far, today had been a real drain for me both mentally and physically. It had been a long long day but it had scarred me for life and all for the right reasons. RIP to all those innocent people who lost their lives at the hands of the cruel and callous Nazi bastards who committed such heinous crimes.

I don't remember at what stage I fell asleep but I was in deep thought as the vivid images of what I'd seen kept showing themselves in black and white. Like an old style projector constantly bringing up old grainy pictures of the past.

CHAPTER 19

Germany (Colditz)

Day 19 - Dresden to Emsdetten via Colditz (Germany)

Date: 24 June 2017
Depart time: 08:30   **Arrive time:** 20:00

Days Mileage: 365 miles
Fuel cost: £61.76 approximately

Route:
Dresden - Colditz - Leipzig - Brunswick - Hannover - Osnabrück - Emsdetten

Roads:
An early run on the motorway to get some miles in, before finding some very good twisty roads near Colditz. Then we used the motorway for the rest of the day.

Border crossing:
None

Weather:
Pleasant riding conditions, approximately 20 degrees during the day, becoming cooler later on.

Countries travelled & Currency:

    Germany   Euro   €

The Days Events - Still bleary eyed

After a pretty poor and restless nights sleep in the Mercure, which was a very nice hotel in Dresden. We were up and ready for breakfast quite early being as it had been such a late arrival. It was a lovely spread for breakfast and quite full even though it was early, the Germans really did know how to look after their customers. There was cold meats and cheese, hot food with bacon, sausages and scrambled eggs, continental type breakfast, fruit, dried fruit and yogurt and much more too. So we tucked in and filled ourselves up ready for the full day ahead, with a few strong coffees to liven us up a little bit before the proceedings began.

After breakfast we headed back to our rooms to finish packing, straight down to the bikes to load them up as they were parked in the garage. We met up and made sure we were fully loaded before we went back up to reception to check out. The bikes were safely garaged the previous night so it didn't take long to get them ready, we hadn't unpacked anything from the previous evening as it was so late when we'd arrived.

Bikes loaded with tank bags and valuables, sat navs switched on and responding to the satellites as we prepared to leave, this time we were heading to Colditz for our finalé of the trip before heading back to Ginge's house in Emsdetten.

We headed out of the garage to the most amazing view of the river with the town as a backdrop, we admired it now because when we'd arrived it had been dark. Our journey started by heading to the outskirts of town and then straight onto the motorway. We wanted to arrive early so that we could be back at Ginge's house by mid afternoon and that was over 400 kms away. As we got closer to our next destination we turned off the motorway and were treated to a marvellous biking road.

I'd forgotten how good the German roads were for riding, twist after twist, corner after corner and bend after bend, beautiful open roads with good views across cropped fields and the wonderful smells of the countryside, just what the doctor ordered for an early start to the day.

Arriving at Colditz

Then from the curvy road and out of nowhere we reached the town sign for Stadt Colditz, Ginge explained why it said Stadt in front of the word Colditz. It was because it had a greater population than a particular number. If it had had a lower population it would simply say Colditz. We were sure at one time in the past, it would have just been the word Colditz. We stopped for a photo and filming opportunity and we were ready to find the castle, well you couldn't actually miss it unless you only looked down at the floor all the time. It was huge and stood out pretty well as we rode further into town.

We made our way up towards the castle, parked our bikes at the famous main gates and had another picture before making our way inside. I waited with the bikes in the car park as Ginge wandered off to see what the crack was. We'd heard that the previous week some guy had his gear stolen from his bike when he was in the castle. Ginge arrived back shortly afterwards with the good news, so we went to reception and they kindly kept our belongings in a small room adjacent to the office for safe-keeping. We booked ourselves onto the next English speaking tour and only had to wait 10 minutes, we didn't waste any time and started snapping away with photos while we waited.

We weren't sure what to expect from the Colditz tour, as the castle had belonged to a family who'd lived there after the war, it had also been turned into a hospital at some stage. It was now a pretty large hostel and obviously wouldn't be in its original state from after the war. We didn't really know what state it would be in or what we would be allowed to see. As we waited we were joined by another 8 people, so the little intimate tour we thought we were going to have had now been gatecrashed by more people. Our tour guide was called Steffi. It was a slow start but she was absolutely fantastic.

A brilliant narrator at Colditz Castle

We were given a general overview of the castle and shown certain areas that had any significance. We were actually taken to various places around the old building and shown where things had been when it was a POW camp, for both officers and prisoners who had escaped from other places. There were old pictures and around the inner grounds were wooden cutouts of prisoners.

The tour was fascinating, this lady was obviously well read and gave us lots of details and stories about what happened and when. She also relayed amusing tales that involved the German guards and prisoners. We were given details of the main goings on and no end of accounts of escapes from a building that nobody could ever escape from - allegedly.

She went on to explain that since the war the people of Colditz did not come to understand the full importance of the place until the early 1990's. Since then it had started to be renovated in part, back to its original state. This place would be well worth a visit in a few years when it had been returned to how it once was. Albeit not the whole place but certain areas that could be transformed as a tour for inquisitive tourists and World War 2 enthusiasts or just those like us who were interested in the past.

We were shown to the attic where a replica life size aircraft/glider was built by two RAF guys in their attempt to fly off the roof to the other side of the River. Their exploits and genius idea came to life a few years ago in the 1990's, when a team requested permission to re-enact the plotted scheme that never got to fruition. The team of people who arrived were given two weeks for the project and they actually managed to fly a plane off the roof, this proved that the idea would certainly have worked given the right conditions. We were amazed, gobsmacked and in awe of the goings on here. We were told, when Colditz was first used as a prison camp, the officers were allowed into the village for a beer at night if they promised to return. Obviously this arrangement didn't last very long when some of them escaped after a cheeky pint.

After the mental trauma and turmoil of Auschwitz, Colditz was a breath of fresh air, we laughed and had lots of fun. We even found a ladder and Ginge re-enacted a breakout, only he was going the wrong way and climbing up towards the castle. The way out was obviously down and he was going up the ladder, it made a good little video sketch that would be part of his video footage for his final day! We were also shown to an area where they had loads of written information on billboards and a small museum area.

The long slog on the motorway

Because we were now well over time and still had a long way to go, we didn't stay the extra few hours to read all the information and look at all the memorabilia. The tour should have only taken a few hours but we had been there for well over 4 hours and it was now mid afternoon. What a brilliant day and I'm sure we'll be having tours there in the future to take in the fantastic roads, along with other famous World War 2 sites in Germany.

So, it was literally hours after we'd expected to leave, it was that interesting we would definitely have to return in the future because there was lots of stuff we hadn't seen. Mainly our tour overran because of our questions and her knowledge. It was Ginge and I asking most of the questions as we'd also done in Auschwitz, Ginge asked most of the questions in German though, as it was easier for the translation so Steffi could understand better. He was even congratulated on the wonderful German that he spoke, which was very nice to hear too. It should be good, as he'd lived there for 30 odd years but I knew people who've lived in Spain and Portugal for years and didn't speak the language at all.

After we'd had a final look around and took a few more pictures it was time to head back to the reception to collect our tank bags and other bits of kit that had been secured for us. We couldn't resist an ice cream as it was pretty warm now and we needed to put some calories in to start the long ride north.

It wasn't long before we were ready to depart on our 350 mile mission up the motorway to get back to Emsdetten. We left Colditz around the same time that we'd expected to arrive at Ginge's place. It was going to be a long ride which would take two full tanks of fuel and we were already feeling a little tired after last night but we ground our teeth and just got on with it.

In true German style, the motorways were fantastic. Fast-flowing and everyone knew how to use them properly. If you got flashed at, you moved over as the person behind was travelling at speed and much faster than you, you were in their way and they were letting you know that they wanted you to move over for them. It worked an absolute treat, it was a pity our nation was so poor at driving on motorways, lane hogging and not moving over if they were driving in the fast lane at the speed limit. It was a pretty fast ride back on the motorway, all the way back to Emsdetten.

On the second fuel break we pulled into the service area for a strong coffee and something to eat. It was a welcome break as we were starting to feel the tiredness creep in. It was times like these, on the last leg of a journey where most accidents happened as you started to switch off as you got closer to home. Ginge was nearly there but I had another big day ahead of me tomorrow to get back home from Germany to England.

The route wasn't very interesting at all, nevertheless we made good time. At times there were crops and plenty of fields and at other times there were lots of trees and dense forests. The Germans were certainly leading the way with alternative energy with loads of wind turbines and solar panel fields. All this to give power to the nation, it was a beautiful country But we were struggling to keep up the concentration at times, because of fatigue and a lack of sleep from the previous night and spending much longer than anticipated at Colditz.

We naturally, without talking about it, took it in turns to lead as it helped to keep up concentration and stopped you from becoming even more tired as concentration dipped. We worked really well together and ensured we were both okay to continue by giving the thumbs up frequently to stay safe for the remaining miles.

The end of the Tour for Ginge

After another full tank of fuel we reached the outskirts of Emsdetten, which was a welcome sight for both of us. We stopped at the garage so that I could get a full tank on board ready for the next morning's early start and then we continued on to Ginge's house for a bit more filming to finish off the tour for the video production in the future.

We finally arrived and when we got into his house I sorted out my gear for tomorrow morning's journey home after grabbing a shower. Ginge headed off out to get some stuff from the shop for breakfast along with some food for tonight. It was a good old 'gyros pita mit pommes', something I hadn't had for many, many years. It was a mouthwatering meal and like any other fast food always seemed better before you had it but when you'd eaten it you felt fat, full and heavy and wished you'd had a healthier option.

Fed and watered we took some video footage and sorted out our remaining SD cards of footage and pictures, had a nice cold glass of beer and toasted the end of Ginge's tour with a large glass of brandy. It wasn't long before we retired and got our weary heads down, I just knew tonight would go far too quickly before it was time for me to head home alone in the morning.

CHAPTER 20

Germany to England

Day 20 - Emsdetten to Redditch via the EuroTunnel (Back to Blighty)

Date: 25 June 2017
Depart time: 06:20   **Arrive time:** 14:10

Days Mileage: 502 miles
Fuel cost: £58.18 approximately

End mileage 42,783 miles
Total travelled 5,285 miles

Route:
Emsdetten (Germany) - Essen - Venlo (Holland) - Eindhoven - Turnhout (Belgium) - Antwerp - Ghent - Bruges - Dunkirk (France) - Calais EuroTunnel - Folkestone (England) - London - Oxford - Birmingham - Redditch

Roads:
Used the motorway all the way home.

Border crossing:
Open borders from Germany through Holland, Belgium and France. Once at the EuroTunnel in France through passport control before getting on the train. I had to show my passport only, vehicle documents were not requested.

Weather:
Started off wet, cold and miserable, brightened up once out of Germany and became clearer and pleasant for the rest of the journey home. Temperature was a pleasant 18-20 degrees.

Countries travelled & Currency:

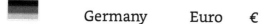   Germany   Euro   €

	Holland	Euro	€
	Belgium	Euro	€
	France	Euro	€
	England	Pound	£

The Days Events - An early departure

After a very good night's sleep I was well rested and ready for an early start. I was up at 05:40 am, well before the alarm was due to go off as I was wide awake. We hadn't needed an alarm clock most days as we were all early risers and didn't have any problems getting out of bed and on with the days proceedings. I took a quick shower to liven up before packing the few bits of kit that was still out from the night before and I headed downstairs without making too much noise.

Ginge had heard me quietly getting ready, he said I walked around like an elephant. Not sure if it was meant as a compliment or not, I took it as one though! So breakfast was prepared for me with a strong cup of coffee whilst I packed the bike ready to leave. I went back indoors to eat breakfast, drink the much needed strong coffee, scrounge a bottle of water and a mars bar to keep me going and I was ready to be on my way. Really it was because Ginge needed his beauty sleep as he looked rough this morning (so did I in all honesty).

I headed off as soon as I could and as I suspected Ginge was going back to his scratcher for another few hours kip. As I said my farewell and started to leave the rain came down, drizzle at first and then heavier the further south I rode. I got out onto the motorway pretty quickly towards Munster and recognised some familiar road signs and names of towns. The rain started to come down and I thought that I should have put my waterproof socks on too! Oh well, I'd had wet feet before and besides it wasn't cold, just raining.

The rain continued all the way through Germany as I travelled south towards Dortmund and then West towards the Venlo and the Dutch border. I didn't look around too much as it was raining hard, I just got my head down and made it to the border in about one and a half hours. Straight across the border and into Holland, it should only take about half an hour or so to transit Holland (I anticipated, going from memory). I thought about getting somewhere near to Antwerp in Belgium before stopping for fuel.

The rain eased and it started to dry up too. I had soggy wet feet but the rest of me was warm and dry, then the fuel light came on and stated that I had 20 miles of fuel left, I wondered if my speed had anything to do with that! Usually it was double that at around 40 miles when it registered low fuel.

I pulled into the next garage because I didn't fancy running out of fuel if I chanced it any further. I went to fill up and had a 5 minute comfort break, when I went to the loo I had to pay to have a pee! When I washed my hands there was some grubby truck driver having a wash and shave in the only sink in the toilet. So I used the ladies toilet on the opposite side to wash my hands, before I headed back to the bike to get on my way.

Using the last Euros on the card

Right then I thought, let's get on with it. I cracked on another 100 miles before I used up the last of my Euros on the fuel card that I'd topped up before I left the UK. I only had €19 left to spend on it, so I best stop in France to do the fuel thing again, to get my money's worth out of the card. It wasn't long before I entered Belgium after I filled up for the first time and then cleared Antwerp. It was always slow around the ring road as it had restricted speed limits there all the time.

Bringing back memories

I then rode towards the direction of Gent and on the way passed a place called Lokeren, it brought back some really good memories and I smiled as I passed the exit. An old friend of mine called Bob Harvey and I had to drive some luggage to Amsterdam for a group of Gurkhas back in the mid 80's in an old Army Bedford 4 tonne truck. We were only young lads in those days and pretty stupid too, we decided on the way back that we would stop off in a town and go and get pissed. I think we threw a dart at a map and the closest place to the dart and the motorway was where we would stop.

To cut a long story short, we had a fantastic night. Got absolutely blind drunk on Belgium's best Pale Ale and slept in the back of the truck we'd abandoned in a housing estate somewhere near the town. Being drunk and daft, we used 20 litre jerry cans as pillows and wondered why we had stiff necks in the morning when we woke up with a massive hangover! Because of the state of us we had to flip a coin to see who was driving first thing in the morning. Fortunately I won the toss and Bob ended up driving the first half of the journey back to Munster. I can't remember what crap excuse we gave for being a day late getting back to camp! The good old days and great times, I reminisced to myself.

Onwards past Gent and then on towards Bruges and then Ostend on the Belgium coast, I turned left and followed the coast road into France. When I got to the Dunkirk area the fuel light came on again, it was giving me less than 20 miles this time. It must be the speed as this hadn't happened anywhere else on the trip except Germany when it was just me and Ginge. So I went off the main drag, filled up with my €19 that was remaining on the euro card and then off again for the final leg of the journey this side of the English channel.

The Channel tunnel

I arrived at the Eurotunnel early and self checked in. They wanted an extra amount of money for the next train so I pressed the no extra charge button. I then went through towards customs, waited in line and then moved on to the next waiting area. There was another 3 bikes in the same lane but it was empty everywhere else, the light turned to green and the barrier went up, so off we all went. We were stopped before we arrived at the train, turned around and guided back to where we had come from and onto another train. This was an hour earlier than planned and we were directed to the next train that was just about to leave.

We got on and within 5 minutes we were on the move and were off back to Blighty, it was the train I didn't want to pay another fare for. We started moving and headed inside the tunnel, it got dark and before long we arrived in the UK half an hour earlier than when we departed France. As we had to change the clocks back an hour because of the time difference. I'd finally made the hour up that I'd lost on the outward journey almost 3 weeks prior but I'd been through a number of time zones since then anyway.

When I was leaving the train I kept my gloves off expecting to go through customs again. As we left I realised there wasn't any passport control here at all, we went straight onto the motorway and that was it. I was the first bike off, following two cars, after I realised my error I popped my gloves on, 'on the move' and made sure I was properly geared up before I hit the M20 northbound.

I arrived at the motorway and straight away, as I expected, I hit slow moving vehicles in the outside lane and the inside lanes were both clear There were also lane hoggers in lane 2 who weren't overtaking anybody! Grrr, 19 easy days riding spent in Europe and then back to the grind of this poor driving style in the UK.

'I'm not moving over' seemed to be the attitude, or 'I'm driving at almost 70 mph so you shouldn't be trying to get past me', or just no consideration to other people. I don't condone speeding but it's not the job of a car driver in the outside lane to determine the speed of all the traffic behind them. But hey, I only had 175 miles to travel until I got home and then I could have a proper rest and relax before getting stuck into work pretty much as soon as I got back.

Then I reached the M25, what a disaster this was turning out to be, a traffic jam for 20 miles and it was filtering all the way to Heathrow. I decided to fill the bike up, just to have a quick comfort break before getting on with the journey again and it did the trick. I was a little more with it after the stop and concentration levels were back, ready to tackle the faster moving M40 northbound towards Birmingham.

Everything went really well, the road was pretty clear for the most part and the rain stayed off until the M42 - welcome home I thought! It wasn't too long before I was off the motorway and heading towards Redditch. As I arrived home, I parked the bike up outside the garage, turned the sat nav off and looked at the trip switch that I'd set in Germany. It said 502 miles, ridden from 06:20 am this morning and it was now 2:10 pm, which wasn't too bad going at all.

That concluded the trip, the weather on a whole for the tour had been fabulous, although it started off pretty wet. The routes we used were absolutely amazing, the journey had certainly given us an insight into what each of the 21 Countries looked like. Albeit as we transited through some of them, we didn't see vast areas.

We got a good feel of what each country looked like from the inside and not on a motorway or a holiday complex that was usually designed to impress. The people we came into contact with had been amazing hosts and ambassadors to their country and were probably not even thinking about it. They were humble and helpful, they cared and were interested in our journey, from where we'd come from, to where we were going to and everything in between!

It had restored my faith in people, it had opened my eyes to what life was like in the many new Countries I'd visited, I was thankful for what I had. It had been a true experience, much more than just a bike adventure and I hoped I could be a much better person because of what I'd seen and experienced in the last 20 days.

What stuck out in my mind the most was the hectic town of Thessaloniki in Greece. Where the young lady, Elena, crossed our paths and went out of her way to help some fellow bikers in their time of need. She was an absolute diamond, I will never forget her kindness and hope one day our paths cross again.

My sincere thanks

My sincere thanks to 'My old mate' Dave Dooling AKA Ginge, for the invitation and the trust that he had in me and for asking me to be part of such a great experience. Also thanks to Mike for his help and support at times when I personally needed it. My final thanks to my wife Carolyn, who understood why I needed to do this trip after the turmoil that we'd both been through the previous two years.

My gratitude to those who have read this book and adventure. I hope it was of interest, entertaining and more than anything else has given you a flavour or even a little nudge, to go and ride your own adventure!

Thank you.

Printed in Great Britain
by Amazon

42948926R00130